P9-CEF-057

**New Directions for
Community Colleges**

Arthur M. Cohen
EDITOR-IN-CHIEF

Florence B. Brawer
Richard L. Wagoner
ASSOCIATE EDITORS

Carrie B. Kisker
Edward Francis Ryan
MANAGING EDITORS

International Reform Efforts and Challenges in Community Colleges

Edward J. Valeau
Rosalind Latiner Raby
EDITORS

Number 138 • Summer 2007
Jossey-Bass
San Francisco

INTERNATIONAL REFORM EFFORTS AND CHALLENGES IN COMMUNITY COLLEGES
Edward J. Valeau, Rosalind Latiner Raby (eds.)
New Directions for Community Colleges, no. 138

Arthur M. Cohen, Editor-in-Chief
Florence B. Brawer, Richard L. Wagoner, Associate Editors

NEW DIRECTIONS FOR COMMUNITY COLLEGES (ISSN 0194-3081, electronic ISSN 1536-0733) is part of The Jossey-Bass Higher and Adult Education Series and is published quarterly by Wiley Subscription Services, Inc., A Wiley Company, at Jossey-Bass, 989 Market Street, San Francisco, California 94103-1741. Periodicals Postage Paid at San Francisco, California, and at additional mailing offices. POSTMASTER: Send address changes to New Directions for Community Colleges, Jossey-Bass, 989 Market Street, San Francisco, California 94103-1741.

SUBSCRIPTIONS cost $80.00 for individuals and $195.00 for institutions, agencies, and libraries in the United States. Prices subject to change. See order form at the back of book.

EDITORIAL CORRESPONDENCE should be sent to the Editor-in-Chief, Arthur M. Cohen, at the Graduate School of Education and Information Studies, University of California, Box 951521, Los Angeles, California 90095-1521. All manuscripts receive anonymous reviews by external referees.

New Directions for Community Colleges is indexed in Current Index to Journals in Education (ERIC).

Microfilm copies of issues and articles are available in 16mm and 35mm, as well as microfiche in 105mm, through University Microfilms Inc., 300 North Zeeb Road, Ann Arbor, Michigan 48106-1346.

CONTENTS

EDITORS' NOTES

In the last quarter century, the international revolution has significantly transformed the sociopolitical, technological, and economic variables that define how countries interact. The effects of globalization are even more acute in the post–September 11 era. Today, globalization has opened borders to the flow of goods, services, information, and people, and in the process it has changed the academic and employment fields by requiring students to know about other cultures as part of their academic, vocational, and occupational education. There is undisputed recognition that the role of education is, in part, to produce internationally literate graduates who can effectively understand the complexities of our modern world.

Community colleges remain on the postsecondary frontlines as they prepare more than half of the nation's college students. Thus it is essential for community colleges to expose their students, faculty, and staff to an international education, which we define as "any form of education that emphasizes the need to understand a variety of perspectives (geographic, ethnic, cultural, class, and gender) by acknowledging similarities, encouraging cross-cultural communication, and respecting and protecting differences among diverse communities" (Raby, 1999, p. 7). This book argues that community colleges must make international education the routine, rather than the exception.

Since the 1960s, community colleges have responded to the need for international educational reform by creating and implementing a variety of programs and practices. Among them are developing faculty and staff exchanges, enrolling international students, offering education abroad programs, and participating in cooperative agreements that provide technical, vocational, and occupational education, workforce improvement, and international trade and development to institutions in other countries. Community colleges have also made significant attempts to internationalize their curricula by incorporating international themes into existing course sequences.

Although efforts to internationalize the community college are growing, many colleges continue to find it difficult to implement international education throughout their entire campus (Green and Siaya, 2005; Romano, 2002). Although there are pockets of excellence, 61 percent of community colleges have a low measure of their overall level of internationalization (Green and Siaya, 2005). Despite the existence of consortia models that offer advocacy and support, many educators still believe that international education is not a key component of the community college's mission. This lack

NEW DIRECTIONS FOR COMMUNITY COLLEGES, no. 138, Summer 2007   © 2007 Wiley Periodicals, Inc.
Published online in Wiley InterScience (www.interscience.wiley.com) • DOI: 10.1002/cc.275

of support is problematic considering that community colleges are the only avenue for some students to acquire the skills necessary to participate in a global knowledge economy. Hence, international education remains for the vast majority of community colleges as marginalized today as it was forty years ago.

Since September 11, 2001, there has been abundant literature on four-year university efforts to initiate international educational reform (U.S. Department of State, 2006; Committee for Economic Development, 2006). However, very few of these publications discuss the community college. Literature on community college internationalization efforts can be found, but it is not as prolific and reflects a pre–September 11 world. It is apparent that a current and comprehensive examination of international education reform in the community college is sorely needed.

This volume seeks to fill this void. The various chapters discuss the peripheral nature of international education and delineate variables that account for college success. Each chapter also lays out unique applications of community college international education and discusses the steps needed to institutionalize international education.

Three common threads are found throughout the various chapters. The first thread examines the role of the new generation of leaders who will be a catalyst for developing, sustaining, and implementing international education. Raby and Valeau suggest general paradigms for historical and philosophical analysis, and in so doing they set the tone for the future of international education. Green defines those elements that are essential for success and identifies some of the barriers to institutionalization. Boggs and Irwin use informal interviews with community college presidents to propose that presidential leadership is the glue for any reform. Hence, international education must be on the agenda for the development of leadership skills for the next generation of community college leaders. Finally, Korbel illustrates how college leaders can use regional and state international education consortia to expand successful institutionalization efforts.

The second thread examines how international education has permeated various components of the college and has made a significant impact over time. Dellow describes how globalization has changed the economy and job market for community college students and how community colleges must now change their technical and occupational programs to remain relevant. Milliron examines this interrelationship further, illuminating what he refers to as the gorilla in our midst and how workforce development programs can respond. Raby defines on- and off-campus forms of internationalizing the curriculum. Emert and Pearson give us a case study in which an assessment of intercultural competencies and international literacy is viewed as an outcome of study abroad participation. Finally, Wells compares a cohort of international faculty with noninternational faculty and calls for greater emphasis on this often-overlooked group in future policies and research.

The final thread explores how international education becomes a catalyst for educational revitalization. Two case studies are presented showing both the success and the problems that can emerge in the constant struggle for institutionalization of international education. Ng's case study of the Peralta Community College District documents the challenges that resulted from internal campus politics and how leadership of one district overcame these problems. Richards and Franco's case study of Kapi'olani Community College illustrates how a single international program was strengthened and transformed into an integrated program that serves as a model for the entire country.

This book suggests a vision for those working to internationalize their community college. A current and comprehensive examination of concepts and methodologies involved in institutionalizing international education reform in the community college is sorely needed. It is our hope the information presented in this *New Directions for Community Colleges* volume fills this void.

Edward J. Valeau
Rosalind Latiner Raby
Editors

References

Committee for Economic Development. *Education for Global Leadership: The Importance of International Studies and Foreign Language Education for U.S. Economic and National Security.* Washington, D.C.: Committee for Economic Development, 2006.

Green, M., and Siaya, L. *Measuring Internationalization at Community Colleges.* Washington D.C.: American Council on Education, 2005.

Raby, R. L. *Looking to the Future: Report on International and Global Education in California Community Colleges.* Sacramento: Chancellor's Office of the California Community Colleges, 1999.

Romano, R. (ed.). *Internationalizing the Community College.* Washington, D.C.: American Association of Community Colleges, 2002.

U.S. Department of State. *U.S. University Presidents Summit on International Education.* Conference Proceedings, Washington, D.C., Jan. 5–6, 2006.

EDWARD J. VALEAU is the president of Hartnell College in Salinas, California, and president of the California Colleges for International Education.

ROSALIND LATINER RABY is director of the California Colleges for International Education and senior lecturer in the College of Education at California State University, Northridge.

1

This chapter traces the historical foundations on which today's community college international programs are based and concludes with strategies for strengthening and expanding the internationalization of community colleges.

Community College International Education: Looking Back to Forecast the Future

Rosalind Latiner Raby, Edward J. Valeau

According to the Commission on the Abraham Lincoln Study Abroad Fellowship program (2005), "What nations don't know can hurt them. The stakes involved are that simple, that straightforward, and that important. For their own future and that of the nation, college graduates today must be internationally competent" (p. 3).

In the post–September 11 era, globalization has acutely transformed the technological, political, economic, and social variables that define how countries interact. To prepare for this changing world, community colleges must produce internationally literate graduates who can effectively navigate the complexities of the modern world. For our purposes, international education is a set of programs and curricula that institutions can employ to globalize students, faculty, and the surrounding communities.

Although most community college leaders accept the basic concepts of international education and appear to understand its significance, collegewide implementation has been difficult to achieve. Despite almost three decades of intense discussion, many educators still do not see international education as a key component of the community college's mission. For example, in a recent study of internationalization in the community college, Green and Siaya (2005) found that international education is still a peripheral activity rather than an institutionalized component. This lack of support is problematic because many community college students do not transfer to a university

NEW DIRECTIONS FOR COMMUNITY COLLEGES, no. 138, Summer 2007 © 2007 Wiley Periodicals, Inc.
Published online in Wiley InterScience (www.interscience.wiley.com) • DOI: 10.1002/cc.276

(the institution that traditionally attends to international education). Thus their only means for acquiring international literacy is through the community college. This chapter traces the historical foundations on which today's community college international programs are based, describes aspects of the debate surrounding international education, and discusses strategies to strengthen the internationalization of community colleges.

Defining International and Global Education

As the field has grown, so does confusion over terms such as *international, global,* and *globalization.* The American Council on International and Intercultural Education (ACIIE) and the Stanley Foundation (1994) define *global education* as an umbrella term that describes a range of activities encompassing intercultural, multicultural, and international education. Although encompassing, this definition fails to delineate the separate and not necessarily conflicting directions these various terms take. Raby (1999) defines *global education* as "education that emphasizes similarities among world cultures and underscores the universality of experience derived from the emergence of new systems, structures, and modalities that combine economic, political and cultural characteristics" (p. 4). *International education* highlights the need to understand a variety of perspectives (geographic, ethnic, cultural, and gender) by acknowledging similarities, and by respecting and protecting differences among multicountry diversities. The inherent difference in these definitions is based on expectations of the social functions of education; the term *international* looks between nations to build multicountry perspectives, and *global* highlights universal perspectives.

In essence, globalization is the phenomenon that exists and that we cannot control, while internationalization is the response that education is making. Moreover, both global and international dimensions exist not only independently but in relation to one another (Raby, 2000); they both seek to accelerate knowledge about and encourage cross-cultural communication to enhance cultural, ethnic, class, and gender relationships among divergent groups.

Historical Foundations of International Education

Since 1967, international education in community colleges has experienced four phases of maturation, beginning with explanations of why internationalizing is important and ending with how it can be implemented (Raby and Tarrow, 1996). By understanding these historical foundations, community college practitioners and scholars can ensure that international education is transformed from a negligible part of the community college to an integral one.

Recognition Phase: 1967–1984. Beginning in 1967, policymakers and administrators began to see community colleges as a plausible receptacle for international education. Between 1969 and 1974, many programs were initiated: Rockland Community College opened a study abroad office in 1969; the College Consortium for International Studies, a tristate consortium, implemented the first cooperative study abroad effort in 1973; California community colleges designed faculty-led study abroad programs in 1974; and Rockland and Brevard colleges adopted an internationalized curriculum in 1974 (Hess, 1982). As well, the first international student support systems emerged in 1974 and international development program collaborations were initiated with the formation in 1976 of a nonprofit consortium called Community Colleges for International Development (CCID). By 1977, three hundred community colleges listed international education as an important college component (Shannon, 1978). Moreover, ACIIE was recognized near the end of this phase. The initial efforts that occurred during this phase set the stage for tremendous growth in the field.

Expansion and Publication Phase: 1980–1990. Phase two witnessed increased adoption and documentation of international education within the community college. In response to a proliferation of published reports arguing that too many students were internationally illiterate, community colleges began receiving national grants to help internationalize the curriculum and prepare students for life in a globalized world. During this period, regional and state consortia developed, and individual college offices were initiated. Policymakers and administrators began to document and disseminate reports that described the benefits of international education. For example, the American Association of Community Colleges (1998) defined the theoretical and philosophical purposes behind community college international education, and several authors (see, for example, Raby and Tarrow, 1996) developed how-to guides that described successful community college international education programs.

Augmentation Phase: 1990–2000. Between 1990 and 2000, community colleges enhanced their existing international efforts by diversifying disciplines for infusion and study abroad, and intensifying international student recruitment. Several programs, such as the University of Oregon's Intercultural Studies Institute, the University of Hawaii's Asian Studies Institute, and UCLA's Teacher Training International Seminars, specifically targeted community college faculty. During this period, ACIIE and the Stanley Foundation held retreats to clarify community college international education goals. Two surveys document the progress that occurred during this period. In 1992, the American Council of Education surveyed sixty randomly selected community colleges and found that 70 percent had international contacts; 50 percent conducted international business, were internationalizing their curriculum, or had study abroad programs; 30 percent had international sister city relations; and 15 percent belonged to international consortia. A decade later, the American Association of Community Colleges (Blair and Phillippe, 2001) surveyed 1,171 colleges and found that

78 percent offered study abroad opportunities, nearly a 30 percent increase since 1995.

Institutionalization Phase: 2000–2007. In the current phase, there is an explicit push to include international education in institutional mission statements and in state and national education policies. There is also an effort to recognize community colleges in national granting programs such as the Lincoln fellowship program, as well as through community college leadership development programs. Moreover, international students have become the nation's fourth largest service sector export, and study abroad programs in community colleges have experienced a 126 percent growth rate, the largest among all postsecondary institutions (Institute for International Education, 2006). In this most recent phase, there has also been recognition of the importance that senior leadership plays in implementing international education programs at the community college. In 2006, the U.S. Department of State, through its University Presidents Summit on International Education, called for a new generation of leadership in the field.

Significance of International Education in Community Colleges

As Bell-Rose and Desai (2006) note, "today's students will be working in a global marketplace and living in a global society. In order to succeed and to become leaders in this new world, they must acquire a far different set of knowledge, skills, and perspectives than previous generations. They must be prepared to trade with, work alongside, and communicate with persons from radically different backgrounds than their own" (p. 2). Clearly, globalization has an impact on our economy and the manner in which political events are conceived and interpreted. In publications dating back to 1980, scholars have identified three rationales for adopting international education: political, economic, and humanistic. We describe these rationales here and add one of our own: academic integrity.

The Political Rationale. Born during the cold war and sustained in the post–September 11 era, the political rationale perceives international education as a pragmatic tool for national security. International study and exploration are critical for undergraduate education because "we can no longer define our national security in military terms alone, for our ignorance of world cultures and languages represent [sic] a threat to our ability to remain a world leader" ("National Security Education Act . . . ," 1991, p. A53). Most political leaders agree that students need international literacy to be politically empowered to actively participate as citizens in a democratic society.

As Secretary of State Condoleezza Rice (2006) recently stated, "Despite the modern prevalence of mobile phones and wireless internet and video conferencing, travel is not less important for diplomacy, it's more important. When you can look a person in the eye as you have a conversation, when you can see the people and the places of foreign countries firsthand, you gain a sense of intimacy and knowledge that does not just come from a phone call or in an e-mail. . . . Travel breaks down stereotypes and makes people quicker to listen and slower to judge. Travel fosters understanding and builds respect and creates a subtlety of opinion." Indeed, several government initiatives have been implemented to support international education for this reason (see Chapter Three).

The Economic Rationale. Since the 1980s, many policymakers have recognized international education as a means to enhance international trade and commerce, and hence to ensure a competitive edge in the world economy. The Committee for Economic Development (2006) asserts that the lack of international literacy skills not only hampers efforts to counter terrorist threats but makes the United States less competitive in the global economy because four out of every five jobs have an international connection. As such, community colleges would be remiss if they did not prepare their students to work, compete, and thrive in this new era.

The Humanist Rationale. Understood through the humanist rationale, international education is a process that helps students understand others in our multicultural society and facilitates greater tolerance and peace. International literacy is contingent on a person's ability to reconcile conflicting ideologies by understanding multiple perspectives and respecting difference. International education produces graduates who are morally adept to function in society. A more empathic and culturally competent citizen benefits society by maintaining cohesive relationships, working with differing types of people, and forming a valuable foundation by which a thriving community can exist.

The Academic Integrity Rationale. The final rationale for international education is based on the assumption that courses and programs not referencing international themes are incomplete. For example, studying nursing without acknowledging health issues that arise from migration or transmission of pandemics is negligent. Studying biology without discussing international environmental impacts is also remiss. Community colleges have always viewed education as a perpetual focus of one's life rather than a singular element defined by occupation, mobility, or socialization. However, faculty are increasingly overwhelmed with students who need remedial work in academic basics, and as a result international efforts are marginalized. To remedy this situation, international literacy must be seen as a key element in lifelong learning.

Philosophical Debate About International Education

Despite the growth of support for international education in the community college, a great debate remains about its value. This debate centers on two philosophical questions: What are the needs of community college students? Who benefits from international education? Although many current community college leaders were once themselves strong faculty supporters of international education, there remain chronic underfunding, lack of support, and elimination of programs. A dichotomy exists between the verbal and actual support that community college leaders give international education.

A Matter of Geography. Since Hollinshead (1936) defined community colleges as institutions that meet the needs of communities within a specific geographic region, a debate has emerged as to what *community* refers to. Applied geographically, a community exists within a specified boundary surrounding the college. The students that the college serves and the academic programs that are offered are directly linked to this geographic space. In this context, international is construed as being in direct competition with the local, and as such only those programs that serve the local economy or university should be supported. Those who take this position argue that international students take seats away from local students and that international experiences are a luxury community college students cannot afford. This view has little merit. By denying access to international programs, community colleges ignore their mission of providing open access to all necessary academic experiences.

When the role of community is seen through the lens of globalization, geographic boundaries become illusionary and the universality of experiences across borders becomes more important. Viewing international education in this way, college leaders understand that their communities support international majors and academic programs. For example, the popularity of international studies and international business classes reflects the community's desire for students to learn about cultures so that they can assist in building a more harmonious and economically prosperous community.

A Matter of Access. The debate about international education in community colleges also involves the issue of access. Some people question whether international programs such as study abroad benefit historically underrepresented community college students or cater to a more privileged group. However, for twenty years community colleges have offered international programs to a broad spectrum of students. Moreover, community colleges offer international education opportunities to a greater proportion of low-income and minority students than in any other postsecondary institutions. It is precisely this open-access philosophy that allows community colleges to help students—including those traditionally excluded from higher education—learn more about the world and participate in the global economy.

Removing or underfunding community college international education programs creates educational inequity. For many students, the choice is not between community college and a four-year institution but instead between the community college and nothing (Cohen and Brawer, 2003). Without international education in community colleges, many students would not have the chance to expand their understanding of the global world or change their perceptions and attitudes about global relationships. The philosophy of open access is placed at risk if four-year college students have access to international programs but community college students do not.

Strategies for Ensuring Institutionalization of International Education

Despite widespread recognition that international education plays an important role in community colleges, several obstacles, notably global terrorism, pandemic influenza, and changes in immigration policy, are causing many to reconsider its benefits. Moreover, tight budgets at many community colleges negatively affect the number of programs that community colleges can support, and decline in the economy influences the number of individuals who can afford to travel abroad. Gains made over past decades, such as international offices, full-time positions, and consortia membership, are constantly being reevaluated and in some cases eliminated. On most community college campuses, support for international programs is limited to the few who have the time and interest to focus on such issues, and their efforts center on immediate rather than broader strategies to institutionalize such programs. As a result, international activities are often confined to events such as festivals or workshops. Ironically, as students and the disciplines they study become more internationalized and the workforce becomes more globalized, the community college is shifting in the opposite direction.

To break this cycle, community colleges must make a genuine commitment to international education that begins with a purposeful plan for educational and policy reform enabling the campus to become fully internationalized (see Chapter Two). There are eight traditionally recognized elements needed for true systemic change to occur (Green and Siaya, 2005; King and Fersh, 1983). Raby and Sawadogo (2005) note that the more of these elements a community college is able to incorporate, the more likely it will institutionalize its international programs.

Clearly Include International Education in College Documents. Inclusion of international education in college documents, such as college mission and annual priorities, extends a mandate that can be drawn on by senior administrators for support. By doing so, there is direct evidence that international education is a significant part of the community college mandate. This articulated commitment is the foundation from which other reforms can emerge.

Ensure Organizational Leadership at All Levels. Visionary leadership and risk taking on the part of college presidents, board members, and faculty members help to prioritize resources and lead reform efforts. The ACIIE and Stanley Foundation reports lay out a blueprint for change, and the ACE Global Education for All project illustrates how it can be done effectively. Leadership always starts with one's own convictions and vision and is followed by articulating the vision clearly, practically, and passionately; committing resources to support the vision; celebrating and making the accomplishments visible; and concretely demonstrating the value added to student experience and institutional mission.

Create Connections Between International Education and Other Programs. The more international education is part of the total college environment, the less it becomes a stand-alone program. International education needs to become a required component of all college committees, hiring mandates, and graduate requirements. For example, St. Louis Community College at Forest Park began with a philosophy that called for funding and an international committee that then lent support for faculty leadership to alter curriculum and mobilize the entire campus.

Create International Committees on Campus. It is critical to include representatives from the entire campus in a committee that is involved in all aspects of campus curriculum and pedagogy. This includes all disciplines and all staff offices—faculty senate, financial aid, and counseling among them. A diverse committee helps institutionalize international education. Equally important is the need to continue mentoring new faculty and administrators to be part of the internationalizing process.

Create a Line Item for International Education in the College Budget. Constant and secure funding is essential for any program to thrive. Changing administrations and college politics often lead to elimination of thriving programs. However, if international education has a dedicated line item in the college budget, this is less likely to occur. College leaders should also actively seek external funding for further support of international initiatives.

Secure Visible Office Space and Staff. The key is to have a physical space with a full-time coordinator who is familiar with current best practices in the field and has adequate clerical assistance to link international education and other college programs.

Provide Counseling Services and Student Advising. Because community colleges offer counseling and student support services, including financial aid, these offices become an important contact area for international education. Staff from these offices must be educated on the benefits and availability of international programs, and they must be encouraged to support international education on all levels.

Create Coalitions with Regional and National Advocacy Groups. Relationships with these groups allow a college to share best practices, form bonds for collaboration, and ensure recognition for international education. The chapter by Korbel details some of the state consortia that use collaboration to secure external funding, and to plan and implement various programs and activities. California Colleges for International Education (CCIE) is such an example, assisting in advocacy and information sharing so that its seventy-eight member colleges have access to best practice standards and the means to collaborate. CCIE offers a biennial conference, quarterly thematic workshops, a monthly online newsletter, and numerous student scholarship and institutional grant programs. There is no need to reinvent the wheel, but there is a need to continue to work together.

Conclusion

In 1983, King and Fersh noted that "international education programs are no longer optional for community colleges, they have become integral" (p. 2). These words have been reiterated by the American Association of Community and Junior Colleges, the ACIIE and Stanley Foundation, and the American Council on Education (Green and Siaya, 2005). Sadly, it is distressing to note that so little has been accomplished since the late 1990s. Although there are beacons of excellence in the field, a significant number of community colleges still have no international educational programs. Moreover, many of the colleges that have programs find fiscal responsibilities continue to wane. Leadership is also inconsistent, as faculty who were once staunch supporters of international education all but ignore it when they are promoted into senior administration. As a result, the peripheral status of international education is reinforced over time.

Finally, there remains no national policy or specified funding that defines, guides, and facilitates implementation of international programs in community colleges. In spite of the problems, community colleges will remain a hotbed for international education. Thus as we move forward into the twenty-first century, we must remember that community college international education is critical and must be protected, especially in times of fiscal uncertainty.

References

American Association of Community and Junior Colleges. "Building Communities: A Vision for a New Century." Report of Commission on the Future of Community Colleges. Washington, D.C.: American Association of Community and Junior Colleges, 1998.

American Council on International and Intercultural Education [ACIIE] and Stanley Foundation. *Building the Global Community: The Next Step*. Conference Proceedings, Warrenton, Va., Nov. 28–30, 1994.

American Council on International and Intercultural Education [ACIIE] and Stanley Foundation. *Educating for the Global Community: A Framework for Community Colleges*. Conference Proceedings, Warrenton, Va., Nov. 15–17, 1996.

Bell-Rose, S., and Desai, V. *Educating Leaders for a Global Society*. New York: Goldman Sachs Foundation, 2006 (http://www2.goldmansachs.com/our_firm/our_culture/corporate_citizenship/gs_foundation/knowledge_center/docs/Educating_Leaders.pdf; accessed Mar. 1, 2007).

Blair, D. P., and Phillippe, K. A. *International Programs at Community Colleges*. Washington, D.C.: American Association of Community Colleges, 2001.

Cohen, A. M., and Brawer, F. B. *The American Community College* (4th ed.). San Francisco: Jossey-Bass, 2003.

Commission on the Abraham Lincoln Study Abroad Fellowship Program. *Global Competence and National Needs*. Washington, D.C.: Commission on the Abraham Lincoln Study Abroad Fellowship Program, 2005 (http://www.lincolncommission.org/Lincoln Report.pdf; accessed Mar. 1, 2007).

Committee for Economic Development. *Education for Global Leadership: The Importance of International Studies and Foreign Language Education for U.S. Economic and National Security*. Washington D.C.: Committee for Economic Development, 2006 (http://www.ced.org/docs/report/report_foreignlanguages.pdf; accessed Mar. 1, 2007).

Green, M., and Siaya, L. *Measuring Internationalization at Community Colleges.* Washington, D.C.: American Council on Education, 2005.

Hess, G. *Freshmen and Sophomores Abroad: Community Colleges and Overseas Academic Programs.* New York: Teachers College Press, 1982.

Hollinshead, B. S. "The Community College Program." *Junior Community College Journal,* 1936, 7(3), 111–116.

Institute for International Education. "Data Tables for Community Colleges." [Datafile.] New York: Institute for International Education, 2006 (http://opendoors.iienetwork. org/?p=25122; accessed Mar. 1, 2007).

King, M., and Fersh, S. "International Education and the U.S. Community College: From Optional to Integral." *ERIC Junior College Resource Review,* Spring 1983.

"National Security Education Act of 1991." *Chronicle of Higher Education,* Dec. 4, 1991, p. A53.

Raby, R. L. *Looking to the Future: Report on International and Global Education in California Community Colleges.* Sacramento: Chancellor's Office of the California Community Colleges, 1999.

Raby, R. L. "Globalization of the Community College Model: Paradox of the Local and the Global." In N. P. Stromquist and K. Monkman (eds.), *Globalization and Education: Integration and Contestation Across Cultures.* New York: Rowman and Littlefield, 2000.

Raby, R. L., and Sawadogo, G. "Education Abroad and Community Colleges." In J. L. Brockington, W. W. Hoffa, and P. C. Martin (eds.), *NAFSA's Guide to Education Abroad for Advisers and Administrators* (3rd ed.). Washington, D.C.: NAFSA, Association of International Educators, 2005.

Raby, R. L., and Tarrow, N. (eds.). *Dimensions of the Community College: International, Intercultural, and Multicultural Perspectives.* New York: Garland, 1996.

Rice, C. "Remarks at the Open Plenary." *U.S. University Presidents Summit on International Education.* Conference Proceedings, Washington, D.C., Jan. 5–6, 2006.

Shannon, W. *A Survey of International/Intercultural Education in Two-Year Colleges.* La Plata, Md.: Charles County Community College, 1978.

ROSALIND LATINER RABY is director of the California Colleges for International Education and senior lecturer in the College of Education at California State University, Northridge.

EDWARD J. VALEAU is president of Hartnell College in Salinas, California, and president of California College for International Education.

2

*This chapter examines variables that make international
education an essential component for community colleges
and identifies barriers to institutionalization.*

Internationalizing Community Colleges: Barriers and Strategies

Madeleine F. Green

There is general consensus that an undergraduate education must produce
graduates who will contribute to civic life both locally and globally; be productive in their work lives; and understand that the fates of individuals,
nations, and the planet are inextricably linked. The United States continues
to need informed and tolerant citizens, members of the workforce who can
function in multicultural environments, and language and area experts
to teach and serve in government. The world needs more—not less—
knowledge and understanding. But there are some important new condi-
tions giving renewed urgency to these needs.

The first is globalization. Americans travel. In 2000, 55 percent of citizens had traveled outside the United States, as had 62 percent of U.S. high
school students (Hayward and Siaya, 2001). In addition, immigration
reached a record high in the 1990s, and technology has made the world
more interconnected. An educational system that pretends the world ends
at our national borders cannot be excellent; a quality education must equip
students to live and work in a globalized and multicultural world.

The second condition is the continued democratization of higher education and the changing nature of students. In 2004, approximately 67 percent
of high school graduates went on to college (NCES, 2006). Of them, only 27
percent are traditional (eighteen to twenty-four years old, financially dependent on their parents, and attending college full-time). As an increasing percentage of high school graduates from diverse cultural backgrounds attend
college, and as more adult students return to higher education they bring with

them differing academic preparations and interests and are likely to attend multiple institutions. This new reality, which may increasingly become the norm at many institutions, calls for reevaluation of the concept of international education. In this changing environment, international education must focus more on classroom learning and less on cocurricular activities and study abroad as well as strengthening connections between our multicultural society in the United States and the larger global context.

The third is the gap between growing national recognition of the need for global and international education and the actual state of internationalization in U.S. higher education. Widespread recognition of this gap should foster both energy and opportunity for higher education institutions to make progress on internationalization.

Community colleges have an important role to play in furthering the internationalization of U.S. higher education. With 52 percent of first-year students enrolled in community colleges, global learning at the postsecondary level must begin there. For those students whose education ends with their community college experience, community colleges are likely to constitute the only formal academic opportunity to learn about other countries, cultures, and global trends. For those students who do transfer to four-year institutions, the two-year institution may still furnish the majority of students' global learning.

Although rhetoric about the urgency of global learning has been abundant in the past quarter of a century, little data about actual institutional practices, such as academic requirements and curricular offerings, were available. Lambert (1989) published some national data on institutional policies and practices, but community colleges were not included in the study. In 2001, ACE conducted a series of studies, surveying two- and four-year institutions, faculty, and students (Siaya and Hayward, 2003); they created an essential empirical foundation for a national dialogue on internationalization. The ACE work is described in here, along with an analysis that examined the differences between institutions that are "highly active" in internationalization and those that are "less active" (Green and Siaya, 2005). After describing these two studies, this chapter discusses barriers to internationalization at community colleges and suggests strategies to address them.

The State of Internationalization in Community Colleges

The ACE survey (Hayward and Siaya, 2001) offers a distinctly mixed picture of internationalization on U.S. campuses, with variation both among and within institutional types. The survey included a stratified sample of 1,501 regionally accredited degree-granting institutions of which 752 responded (a 50 percent rate). Two hundred thirty-three of the 552 community colleges that were surveyed responded (42 percent).

The study looked at seven dimensions of internationalization: stated institutional commitment, academic requirements, organizational structure,

funding, communication structure, faculty opportunities, and student opportunities. Although ACE was cautious about comparing two-year and four-
year institutions, the study showed that community colleges were less active
in all of these areas. For example, 23 percent of community colleges had an
internationally focused course as part of the general education requirement,
compared to slightly more than half of four-year institutions. Community colleges were also less likely than their four-year counterparts to seek external
funding for internationalization, have foreign language graduation requirements for students, or offer study abroad programs. On the other hand, they
were more likely to hold faculty workshops on internationalization.

Within the community college category, 25 percent of institutions men-
tioned internationalization or international education in their mission statement; 16 percent listed internationalization as one of their top five strategic
plan priorities; 44 percent had a campuswide task force that worked to
advance internationalization on their campus; and 38 percent actively
sought external funding to support internationalization. Furthermore, 33
percent of the colleges earmarked funds to recruit international students;
12 percent had at least one office dedicated exclusively to administering
international education activities; 38 percent administered study abroad programs; and 36 percent offered workshops to faculty on internationalizing
the curriculum (Hayward and Siaya, 2001).

A follow-up study, *Measuring Internationalization at Community Colleges*
(Green and Siaya, 2005), analyzed the same survey data to create an internationalization index. An overall internationalization score was created for
community colleges, using a five-point scale: zero, low, medium, medium-
high, and high. The majority of community colleges (61 percent) scored low
as a measure of their overall level of internationalization. All colleges scoring in the top 40 percent were considered highly active in international education for the purposes of this study. Within this group of highly active
community colleges, most scored medium (33 percent). Only 5 percent
scored medium-high, and none scored high. The study compared differences between highly active and less active institutions. Scores were also
developed for six dimensions of internationalization using the same five-
point scale. (The seven dimensions of the questionnaire were combined and
relabeled, resulting in six dimensions for this index.) The dimensions were:

1. Articulated commitment (the extent to which an institution has written statements or established policies supporting internationalization)
2. Academic offerings (availability of for-credit academic offerings with
   an international focus, including foreign language learning, internationalized general education requirements and course offerings, and
   study abroad)
3. Organizational infrastructure (the resources institutions make available
   to support and promote internationalization, including physical facili-
   ties, human resources, and communications and technological support)

4. External funding (institutional efforts to seek and succeed in receiving external funds specifically earmarked for international education programs and activities)
5. Institutional investment in faculty (including professional development opportunities to help faculty increase their international skills and knowledge and internationalize their courses)
6. International students and resources (the number of international students on campus and the amount of funding used to recruit international students, educate students abroad, and offer internationally focused campus activities)

There were noticeable differences between the institutions that were considered highly active and those that were less active. Highly active institutions were much more likely to highlight international education in their recruitment literature than less-active colleges (65 percent compared to 14 percent); have policies that enable students to study abroad without delaying their graduation (75 percent compared to 15 percent); administer study abroad programs for undergraduate credit (66 percent compared to 19 percent). Highly active institutions were also more likely to have an infrastructure to support internationalization: 76 percent of highly active institutions had a campuswide task force exclusively devoted to internationalization, compared to 23 percent of less-active institutions; and 92 percent had an office to administer international education programs, compared to 41 percent of the less-active institutions. Finally, highly active institutions were more likely to seek external funds for international education (78 percent compared to 10 percent) and to earmark funds for regular, ongoing international activities on campus (72 percent compared to 18 percent).

In spite of the differences between highly active and less-active institutions, it is important to note that the research reveals only a minority of community colleges making significant efforts to internationalize. Given the important role that community colleges play in introducing college students to global learning, they need to ramp up their efforts on this front. Although real obstacles to institutionalizing international education exist, there are also many opportunities. The next sections discuss both the obstacles and the strategies to address these obstacles.

Barriers to Internationalization at Community Colleges

ACE's work with all types of higher education institutions suggests that the barriers to internationalization are not sector-specific. Thus community colleges experience the same obstacles as other institutions, and the differences are usually a matter of degree. The major barriers to internationalization are both institutional (internationalization is not supported by the institution's mission, policies, strategies) and individual (faculty and students do not have the expertise or interest needed to participate in internationalization).

Institutional Leaders Do Not View Internationalization as Relevant. The perception that institutional leaders do not view international education as relevant is perhaps the most powerful obstacle to internationalization at the community college. Given the local roots and focus of community colleges, it is not surprising that institutional leaders, board members, and community members may not value global learning as much as the more immediate tasks of workforce development and teaching basic skills. But if leaders take a broader vision, they can connect the global to the local, recognize the relevance of global learning to institutional and community outreach, and understand its utility in preparing students for citizenship and for jobs in a multicultural workplace. For this to happen, however, institutional leaders must articulate this vision compellingly and engage stakeholders in a discussion of the potential benefits of internationalization.

Lack of Institutional Strategy. Few institutions have an internationalization strategy; their strategic plan is likely to be silent on the topic. Institutions often confine their strategy to one or two discrete activities, such as recruiting more international students or increasing the number of students studying abroad. Rarely do institutions consider internationalization a sufficient priority to devote a section of the institutional plan to it, or to develop a separate plan that addresses the several dimensions of internationalization. Moreover, few institutions use a standing or ad hoc group to think strategically; most often, internationalization task forces or committees are charged with coordinating or enhancing the activities that already exist. A better institutional strategy includes a well-articulated plan of activities that connects student learning outcomes with the activities intended to produce them (Olson, Green, and Hill, 2005). Thus community colleges seeking to produce "globally competent" students need to define what this means and look across their various internationalization activities to determine the extent to which they actually support those goals. In other words, the intentional linkages among institutional goals, student learning outcomes, and institutional programs and activities must be the core of an institutional strategy for international education.

International Programs and Activities Are Fragmented. Over the past few years, ACE has worked with more than twenty institutions conducting a review of internationalization, including six community colleges, two of which are profiled elsewhere in this volume. Most of the participating institutions were pleased to see the pockets of internationalization that exist across their campus or district. However, the reviews also highlighted the extent to which these initiatives existed independently of each other. Academic departments and other units on campus were often unaware of internationally focused expertise or programs elsewhere in the institution, and international initiatives remained largely in their separate silos. The result was missed opportunities for synergy among the various programs and resources.

Lack of Funding. The problem of insufficient resources exists on nearly every community college campus and is the most frequently cited barrier to change. Funding for course development and international travel is in short supply. Insufficient funding is further exacerbated by the marginal status of internationalization on most campuses. Budget cuts hit travel first, with international travel being especially vulnerable. The good news is that even small investments can have a significant impact. Grants for course development, partial funding for faculty travel, and release time for project and curriculum development usually have modest costs and significant returns.

External funding can also supply essential discretionary dollars to support faculty activities. Title VI and other federal programs are a key source of funding for faculty development, research abroad, and curricular revision. Although federal and other external funding can offer much-needed help, they lend support only to institutional efforts. External funds cannot create a strategy or commitment where one does not exist. Reliance on external funding also jeopardizes continuing internationalization activities after the funding ends.

Global Learning Must Be Focused in the Classroom. Too frequently, internationalization is seen as occurring outside the classroom—in campus events or education abroad. However, the majority of community college students have significant obligations that preclude them from studying abroad; their learning takes place largely in the classroom. Thus for community colleges and other institutions serving adult, working, and part-time students, internationalization of the curriculum is critical. To participate in this work, faculty must have the expertise and the inclination. Unfortunately, not all faculty have both. As a result, faculty development is vital. Institutions should offer workshops for faculty that enrich their knowledge base as it relates to international, intercultural, and global knowledge. However, internationalizing the curriculum is not a trivial undertaking. Adding an internationally focused module or reading may not require a significant restructuring of a course, but revamping the American history survey course so that U.S. history is put in a more global context can require significant rethinking on the part of the instructor. Community colleges face a special challenge in working with faculty to internationalize the curriculum because of their high proportion of part-time faculty. Schools such as St. Louis Community College at Forest Park have addressed this issue by addressing internationalization in the orientation for new part-time faculty and encouraging them to attend the workshops offered on internationalization.

Individual Attitudes. Not all barriers to internationalization are institutional; sometimes the lack of movement can be explained by individual, rather than organizational, barriers. Individual motivation to be involved in internationalization depends considerably on one's attitude toward international and intercultural learning. Some faculty may be personally interested; others perceive such learning to be extraneous to their personal and academic goals. The value they place on international and intercultural learning is often correlated with their personal experiences. Faculty members may consider international learning irrelevant, doubting that individuals studying a particular field would ever need global competencies and believing that technical expertise in the subject is the only content of importance. Other instructors may hold the view that everyone speaks English and that the world is becoming culturally homogeneous through globalization, thus eliminating the need to study other languages or cultures. Or they may believe that the campus experience is already sufficiently internationalized thanks to the high number of first-generation immigrants or international students on campus.

Personal Knowledge and Expertise. Because academic expertise is a central source of satisfaction and self-worth for faculty, willingness to engage in internationalization depends on their personal capacities and experiences with other cultures and languages. Those who were born into another cultural tradition, in another country or within the United States, are likely to have their interests fueled by their own cultural and linguistic heritage. Faculty who have spent time abroad are also likely to have developed cultural and linguistic competencies, and those with formal international training in graduate school are likely to continue carrying out internationalized research and teaching. At the other end of the continuum are individuals who have no international experience or interest in engaging in international learning or teaching. Such faculty may be more inclined to articulate concerns about internationalization or ignore it in their own professional lives. Their opposition or indifference may be grounded in concern about their own personal capacity to contribute meaningfully to internationalization efforts, or about their role in a changed institutional environment.

Internationalized Mind-Set. Paige and Mestenhauser (1999) discuss an internationalized mind-set, one that is integrative, intercultural, interdisciplinary, comparative, transferal, contextual and global, as a key factor in successful internationalization of a community college. Faculty members with an international mind-set draw on knowledge from diverse settings, cultures, and languages to internationalize the curriculum; use integrative skills such as translating, synthesizing, and connecting; and are adept at identifying the cultural influences that shape these examples. As faculty use interdisciplinary or comparative approaches, they must grapple with issues such as how disciplines are culture-bound and the limits of comparative analysis. Developing an internationalized mind-set can be particularly challenging, since it requires examining assumptions underlying the discipline and developing or refining a set of intellectual skills different from those emphasized in their original graduate training and by their professional disciplinary association.

Overcoming These Barriers

Although many of the obstacles discussed in the preceding sections are difficult to overcome, several community colleges have done so successfully. Here are strategies for overcoming community college barriers to institutionalizing international education.

Ensure Active Leadership. Not surprisingly, the institutions that are most successful in internationalization have presidents and chief academic officers who are ardent supporters and public champions of internationalization. These senior leaders send consistent and repeated messages to faculty, staff, students, and external stakeholders that internationalization is vital to the community, and to the institution's vibrancy. Sustained attention is essential; making internationalization part of the fabric of an institution is a decade-long undertaking. Verbal support and encouragement is necessary but not sufficient. To make the rhetoric real, leaders must help make internationalization happen by allocating or raising funds to support it, removing barriers, and letting faculty and staff take charge. Though enthusiasm for a given program or initiative is never universal on any campus, widespread faculty and administrative leadership is essential in creating institutional energy, imparting legitimacy, and achieving broad participation.

Create a Strategic Framework for Action. Colleges and universities are skilled at making changes at the margins. But internationalization requires more than the addition of a general education requirement or an increase in the number of international students. Each initiative is only a piece of a larger whole. Internationalization is a change that is both broad—affecting departments, schools, and activities across the institution—and deep, expressed in institutional culture, values, policies, and practices. It requires articulating explicit goals and developing coherent and mutually reinforcing strategies to reach those goals. An internationalized campus has more than a series of courses or programs that promote international learning; it links them together to create an intentional learning environment and to foster a set of global learning experiences for as many students as possible.

Use Available Assets. Community colleges have tremendous assets that can be used to promote internationalization. The first asset is the student body. For example, Northern Virginia Community College, St. Louis Community College at Forest Park, and Kapi'olani Community College have highly diverse student bodies that include many recent immigrants (in the case of Northern Virginia and St. Louis) or a majority of students that bring along a linguistic and cultural heritage (Kapi'olani). These students can make an enormous contribution to campus internationalization through the perspectives and experiences they bring to the classroom, and their ties to the local community.

Similarly, the local community can give significant support to internationalization. For example, students can undertake language study and service learning projects with cultural and ethnic groups in the community.

Local businesses with global interests (or multinational corporations located in the community) can offer internships and financial support. Some community colleges support local and international workforce development and training partnerships. Furthermore, many institutions participate in state and local trade delegations, demonstrating the role that higher education plays in local economic development in the global context.

Ensure Faculty Development and Engagement. As noted in the preceding section, faculty are the institutional actors who make internationalization a reality. Once faculty members develop firsthand international experience, their interest and enthusiasm grow quickly. An investment in faculty development pays off in faculty support for international education, in the enthusiasm they communicate to students, and in their own teaching. Community colleges may have few resources to devote to international travel for faculty; nonetheless, even small grants set aside from the overall faculty development fund go a long way. As ACE has found, community colleges offer workshops to help faculty internationalize (Hayward and Siaya, 2001). Such programs can be offered in collaboration with other institutions at relatively low cost. Some community colleges have used a combination of external and institutional funding for faculty development. Tidewater Community College, for example, has secured external funding from federal and state sources to run study tours for faculty and curriculum development seminars focusing on regions of the world. Similarly, Kapi'olani Community College has secured foundation funding for Japanese language and study abroad programs.

Commit to Meeting Student Needs. Some students may perceive global learning as irrelevant to their interests or career, or as simply boring. For example, language classes that are not using innovative pedagogy or that envision all students as prospective language and literature majors rather than as travelers or professionals are a notorious deterrent to language study. Thus, a course such as Spanish for Nurses is likely to elicit more interest than a general language course. Similarly, institutions that do not offer study abroad tailored to the budgets, interests, and schedules of their students are unlikely to appeal to students.

Providing Supporting Structures and Resources. As noted earlier in the chapter, the most frequently cited reason for inaction in higher education is lack of funding. Indeed, there is never enough money available for all worthy innovations, and internationalization does make a claim on resources. But almost none of the higher education institutions ACE has worked with had generous funding available for internationalization initiatives; most relied on a combination of reallocation of existing resources— often incrementally and over time—and modest external funding. These funds went a long way in supporting good ideas and curricular reforms.

Community colleges that have an office to oversee internationalization efforts or a fairly senior professional to head it are clearly at an advantage. Having a point-person brings a focal point for information and coordination and helps promote synergy among the disparate activities. Without this consistent leadership and support, internationalization risks being totally dependent on the interest and energy of a few committed individuals.

Conclusion

Community colleges have a vital role to play in ensuring that all students in U.S. postsecondary education can function as effective citizens of their community and of the world, and that they are equipped for tomorrow's workforce challenges. To achieve this potential, community colleges need to be intentional and strategic in giving students learning opportunities—largely in the classroom—that promote an understanding of other cultures and histories and the global forces that shape the daily lives and futures of our communities. For many colleges, a focus on internationalization requires a new mind-set, one that connects the agendas of diversity within the United States to the larger global context, that forges more intentional links between the local and the global. It also requires leadership, faculty engagement, resources, and structures to support this effort.

References

Green, M., and Siaya, L. *Measuring Internationalization at Community Colleges.* Washington, DC: American Council on Education, 2005.

Hayward, F., and Siaya, L. *A Report on Two Surveys About Internationalization.* Washington, D.C.: American Council on Education, 2001.

Lambert, R. *International Studies and the Undergraduate.* Washington, D.C.: American Council on Education, 1989.

National Center for Education Statistics. "Table 181: College Enrollment and Enrollment Rates of Recent High School Completers, by Race and Ethnicity." *Digest of Education Statistics Tables and Figures 2005.* Washington, D.C.: U.S. Department of Education, National Center for Education Statistics, 2006 (http://nces.ed.gov/programs/digest/d05/tables/dt05_181.asp; accessed Mar. 1, 2007).

Olson, C., Green, M., and Hill, B. *Building a Strategic Framework for Comprehensive Internationalization.* Washington, D.C.: American Council on Education, 2005.

Paige, M. R., and Mestenhauser, J. A. "Internationalizing Educational Administration." *Educational Administration Quarterly,* 1999, *35*(4), 500–517.

Siaya, L., and Hayward F. *Mapping Internationalization on U.S. Campuses: Final Report 2003.* Washington, D.C.: American Council on Education, 2003.

MADELEINE F. GREEN *is vice president for international initiatives at the American Council on Education.*

This chapter focuses on issues that community college leaders constantly grapple with to ensure that their graduates are globally educated and able to work and succeed in an independent and complex world. It also describes major obstacles that limit and confine international education and suggests strategies to overcome these obstacles.

What Every Community College Leader Needs to Know: Building Leadership for International Education

George R. Boggs, Judith Irwin

There was a time when the United States could be comfortable knowing that it controlled the resources needed to sustain a high quality of living, that our geographic isolation protected our national security, and that no other nation could compete with us economically. But the world has changed. The twenty-first century ushers in a new era, with the highest level of global interconnectedness in human history. As Rufus Glasper, chancellor of the Maricopa Community College District in Arizona, notes, the United States has more than twenty trade agreements with other countries and regions and is a member of the World Trade Association. More than a quarter of the U.S. domestic product is trade-related, supporting more than twelve million American jobs, including one in five of our manufacturing workers. The United States is the world's largest importer of merchandise and commercial services, and the second largest exporter of merchandise. U.S. companies have become international as they realize that the vast majority of the world's consumers and purchasing power lie outside of our borders.

America's community colleges, now educating nearly half of all undergraduate students, have a significant role to play in preparing students to live in an increasingly global society and economy. Moreover, U.S. government officials have recognized that community colleges can promote national security and world peace by helping educate students from developing countries and by promoting the study of foreign languages (Bush, 2006). As Eduardo Padron, the president of Miami-Dade College in Florida, has suggested,

"International education must be a high priority. The world is populated by far too much misunderstanding, hatred, and violence. Education demands that the learner clarify his or her attitudes and perceptions, replacing fixed notions with genuine openness. This is the bounty offered by higher education, the potential to transcend the narrow ideas that set people against one another."

This chapter focuses on issues that community college leaders constantly grapple with to ensure that their graduates are globally educated and able to work and succeed in an independent and complex world. It also describes major obstacles that limit and confine international education and suggests strategies to overcome these obstacles. To prepare for this chapter, the authors sent a brief questionnaire to community college leaders who are committed, dedicated, and knowledgeable about international education. The leaders were asked to discuss the importance of international education; their campus's international education components; major obstacles to implementing these components; and strategies leaders can use to overcome obstacles and advance international education. All quotes are derived from these interviews.

Building the Global Community on Community College Campuses

Community colleges have a responsibility to acknowledge global understanding and communication as integral to their mission. Community college governing boards and chief executives, as well as their administrators, faculty, and staff who oversee programs and services, must not only embrace global education but also challenge their communities to understand its importance. To expand students' knowledge and awareness of cultural differences, and to develop necessary skill sets to operate in a changing world, community colleges now offer programs that support a more international view. The curriculum is expanding to include global components: recruitment programs seeking international students are growing, study abroad programs for community college students are developing, and faculty and staff exchanges are being encouraged and implemented. However, as Dennis Harkins, the provost at Georgia Perimeter College, suggests, significant barriers to building an effective and integrated program still exist. Notable are lack of support from trustees, faculty, staff, and the community; limited resources; insufficient student mobility; and inability to understand the significance of international students on campus, culturally and economically.

Leadership. Any component of an organization that reports to a senior administrator is considered to be more important than those that do not. If an office or department reports to a lower-level administrator, it is seen as less of a priority for the organization's leadership. Therefore, responsibilities to develop, administer, and oversee international education must come from the senior administration. Further, it is up to these senior leaders to establish a network that focuses all international activities into a comprehensive center, and to ensure adequate staffing to coordinate all international activities; the staff position should report to either the provost or the president. This centralization helps increase communication, decrease duplication, and promote overall success. Focusing all international-related activities in a comprehensive center and having a direct reporting line to the president or chancellor is necessary for incorporation of the international program into the campus.

Mission and Community Acceptance. Colleges must develop a new mind-set toward international education that emphasizes inclusiveness. A clear global learning mission statement is essential if administrators, faculty, students, community residents, and leaders are to develop strategic goals to better prepare all stakeholders to be globally engaged. As Margaret Lee, president of Oakton Community College in Illinois, notes, the concept of global education must be "woven through our mission, vision, and values statements. We use these statements to drive planning, budgeting, and decision making." If the college leaders do not make global education a priority, it will not become one.

Creating such an environment, however, is tempered and challenged by the reality of constricted attitudes, isolationist views, and lack of understanding that diversity and multiplicity are essential to surviving in the twenty-first century. Overcoming this obstacle is only the first step; there are numerous other barriers that can sabotage and limit an effective program. The community needs to understand and accept the importance of travel and study abroad, embrace international students, and recognize that diversity is the key to expansion and success.

Resources and Faculty and Staff Support. The lack of dedicated resources can also be a major stumbling block. Funds are essential if a college is to hire faculty and staff to develop new programs and expand opportunities, send faculty overseas, offer study abroad programs, and develop new infrastructures for international students. Even more important than resources are dedicated faculty and staff who believe in the value of incorporating global ideas into the college's mission and goals. Campuswide integration is crucial to avoid the perception that there are inadequate funds to sponsor initiatives and scholarships, as well as the perception that international operations are focused on fun activities.

Mobility of Students to Study Abroad. According to the American Association of Community Colleges (2006), community colleges educate 45 percent of the nation's undergraduates. However, the Institute for International Education (2006) suggests that fewer than five thousand community college students study abroad annually. Time and money are typically the most significant barriers that prevent community college students from participating in study abroad programs. These students often lack mobility because of work commitments, family and financial obligations, fear of leaving their community, and the cost associated with the program.

To address these barriers, colleges are developing more flexible programs and helping students find funding. For students who face mobility issues, community colleges are designing three- to six-week programs in which students can study the language, culture, or biology of another country. Although short-term programs can be limiting, they bring a global awareness that otherwise would be lacking. Other institutions are raising funds, establishing scholarships, and using federal aid to help students pay for study abroad programs. For example, some colleges help students obtain the U.S. Department of State Gilman Scholarship, which furnishes resources to outstanding American undergraduates (including community college students) who otherwise could not afford to study abroad.

International Students at Community Colleges. International students play an important role in internationalizing the campus. Interacting with students from other countries gives U.S. students a window to the world. Class discussions are richer, interactions become cross-cultural, and opportunities to host students in local homes deepen understanding of both the differences and the commonalities among people. The presence of international students reduces insularity among students, faculty, staff, and the local community—thereby counteracting provincialism and xenophobia. In addition, international student enrollments bring excess revenues to the college and local economy. During the 2005–06 academic year, international students and their dependents contributed $13.5 billion to the U.S. economy. Although this figure covers monies spent by five hundred thousand international students, eighty-three thousand (16.6 percent) attended community colleges (Institute for International Education, 2006).

At the same time, community colleges are an ideal setting for international students to begin their postsecondary education. In many other countries, student mobility is not encouraged; foreign two-year institutions typically offer vocational or technical education. In the United States, community colleges constitute a less intimidating environment, with smaller classes and increased faculty interaction. International students have access to intensive English programs, excellent counseling options, and the ability to transfer their credits to a university. The college is also close to their community, giving international students an opportunity to experience American community life.

Although it is clear that international students both contribute to and benefit from the community college, recruitment of international students is a constant challenge. To effectively recruit and retain international students, community colleges must have an infrastructure that affords international students access to housing, medical care, insurance, transportation, counseling, advising, and socialization. These support services are essential for the retention and success of international students. As Sean Fanelli, the president of Nassau Community College in New York, points out: "By providing services to our international students, we can learn how to better serve our own diverse population. International students also provide the opportunity for enrollment growth within less popular majors, are good for demographics, and help with overcoming levels of insularity in our community and student body. In many instances, international students' high standards of performance spark achievement in domestic students."

New Directions for Community Colleges • DOI: 10.1002/cc

U.S. Government Initiatives Focused on International Student Recruitment

Having discussed the issues community college leaders grapple with, we turn for the remainder of this chapter to discussion of how the federal government is working with colleges to expand international education. In 2006, the U.S. Departments of State and Education joined forces to host a U.S. University Presidents' Summit on International Education, perhaps the first convening of higher education and government on such a large scale. Although billed as a university presidents' summit, 14 of the 113 attendees were community college presidents and chancellors.

The overall theme of the summit was to renew and energize the partnership between government and higher education in international education, with emphasis on the promotion of world peace and understanding. President George W. Bush (2006) opened the summit with his proposal for a National Security Language Initiative. The president made the case that deficits in foreign language learning negatively affect our national security, diplomacy, law enforcement, and intelligence communities, and they have a negative impact on cultural understanding. In a follow-up session, Secretary of State Condoleezza Rice (2006) outlined her goals for international education: expansion of the Fulbright and Gilman exchange programs; cultivation of exchange relationships with such countries as China, India, Iraq, and Afghanistan; increasing international diversity within our colleges and universities; and continued improvement of visa policies. Secretary of Education Margaret Spellings (2006) continued the conversation by proposing partnerships between higher education and K–.12 schools for language training, research, and an online clearinghouse for language study.

Finally, Undersecretary of State for Public Diplomacy Karen Hughes (2006) argued that higher education must engage, exchange, educate, and empower international students. According to Hughes, educational institutions have the capacity to increase the number of international students they host, and in so doing they would make the United States the world's destination for higher education. She also indicated that the State Department plans to sponsor trips for college and university presidents to educate young people in other countries about American higher education. The first of these trips was led by Secretary Spellings to Asia in November 2006 and included two community college presidents. Undersecretary Hughes also used the summit to discuss her interest in expanding study abroad programs for students, especially women, from certain developing countries (Brazil, Egypt, Indonesia, Pakistan, South Africa, and Turkey).

Conclusion

Community college leaders increasingly recognize that global awareness is a necessity for students to be competent and able to function in an increasingly complex world. The strength of our changing communities depends on American citizens' ability to understand and interact with the peoples of the world. To emphasize their commitment to international education, the American Association of Community Colleges and the Association of Community College Trustees (2006) issued *Building the Global Community: A Joint Statement on the Role of Community Colleges in International Education.* This statement offers suggestions on how to promote global competency, as well as advocating for study abroad and recruitment of international students.

Community colleges are the access point for higher education for many citizens. In that, it is critical that they assume a leadership role in the global education of their communities. Community colleges can affect large segments of our citizenry with information about and awareness of other cultures, traditions, and languages. As the world becomes more complex and fractured, the U.S. community college system can be the cornerstone to ensure that diversity, tolerance, and mutual respect are valued national assets.

References

American Association of Community Colleges. *Community College Fact Sheet.* Washington, D.C.: American Association of Community Colleges, 2006 (http://www.aacc.nche. edu/Content/NavigationMenu/AboutCommunityColleges/Fast_Facts1/Fast_Facts.htm; accessed Mar. 2, 2007).

American Association of Community Colleges and Association of Community College Trustees. *Building the Global Community: A Joint Statement on the Role of Community Colleges in International Education.* Washington, D.C.: American Association of Community Colleges, 2006 (http://www.aacc.nche.edu/Content/NavigationMenu/Resource Center/Services/International/AACCACCT_Joint_Statement.pdf; accessed Mar. 2, 2007).

Bush, G. W. "Remarks to the U.S. University Presidents Summit on International Education." *U.S. University Presidents Summit on International Education.* Conference Proceedings, Washington, D.C., Jan. 5–6, 2006.

Hughes, K. "Under Secretary of State for Public Diplomacy and Public Affairs at the Summit of U.S. Presidents on Higher Education." *U.S. University Presidents Summit on International Education.* Conference Proceedings, Washington, D.C., Jan. 5–6, 2006.

Institute for International Education. *Open Doors: Report on International Educational Exchange.* New York: Institute for International Education, 2006 (http://opendoors. iienetwork.org/; accessed Mar. 1, 2007).

Rice, C. "Remarks at the Open Plenary." *U.S. University Presidents Summit on International Education.* Conference Proceedings, Washington, D.C., Jan. 5–6, 2006.

Spellings, M. "Delivered Remarks at the U.S. University Presidents Summit on International Education." *U.S. University Presidents Summit on International Education.* Conference Proceedings, Washington, D.C., Jan. 5–6, 2006.

GEORGE R. BOGGS *is president and chief executive officer of the American Association of Community Colleges.*

JUDITH IRWIN *is director of international programs and services of the American Association of Community Colleges.*

NEW DIRECTIONS FOR COMMUNITY COLLEGES • DOI: 10.1002/cc

4

This chapter describes how globalization is changing the U.S. economy and the job market for community college students and discusses the skills students need to participate in a globalized world.

Transcendence and Globalization: Our Education and Workforce Development Challenge

Mark David Milliron

Daniel Simons, a neuroscientist at the University of Illinois, explores perception, attention, and memory with some pretty intriguing methods. In one experiment, he asks an audience to watch a video of two three-member basketball teams, one wearing white shirts, the other black. In the video, each group passes their team's ball among themselves, all the while weaving back and forth among the other team. It is a pretty confusing little scene. The audience's job is to count the number of times the white-shirt team members pass their basketball to one another. At the end of the exercise, Simons begins the questioning: Who counted sixteen passes? seventeen? eighteen? But then he asks, who saw the gorilla? Yes, that's right, who saw the gorilla? Most of the people who participate in this exercise, 70–80 percent, fail to notice that halfway through the video a man in a gorilla suit walks across the room, stops smack in the middle of the passing teams, turns to face the camera, beats his chest, then walks through to the other side. Most people absolutely miss the primate prancing across the screen. When shown the scene again, they cannot believe they missed it; they are confused, sometimes mad, and other times absolutely certain there are two videos.

The gorilla video demonstrates perceptual blindness. This concept is related to the fact that we all have cognitive structures that make up our brain patterns; they are literally the building blocks of how we think. These structures are based on key factors such as life experience and learning.

NEW DIRECTIONS FOR COMMUNITY COLLEGES, no. 138, Summer 2007 © 2007 Wiley Periodicals, Inc.
Published online in Wiley InterScience (www.interscience.wiley.com) • DOI: 10.1002/cc.279

Usually, our cognitive frameworks help us survive and thrive in the world. However, if objects come up that do not fit into the structures we have created, we can end up literally blind to them. It is more likely to happen when we are focused and on task. Trying harder in these cases is of little use; it may actually make things worse.

Simon's basketball experiment shows that sometimes, especially at key transformational points in our personal, business, national, and international lives, we literally have to think differently—almost restructure our world from the inside out. But we have to be patient because many people in our circle, on our team, in our college, in our community, and in our country, still do not see the gorilla. Even after it is pointed out, they think it is a trick. We have to patiently bring them along, help them see the change at hand, and prepare them for a different future.

In case you have not noticed, the globalization gorilla is in the room. We are experiencing a tumultuous time of transformation in industry and society. I offer here a sense of the scope of this global transformation, the skills that will become essential as a result, and a call to action for community colleges whose purpose is to prepare students and communities to earn and learn in this new world.

Scope of the Global Transformation

Thomas Friedman (2005) sums up the scope of the change at hand in what is becoming one of the most repeated phrases in business journals and political circles: *The World Is Flat*. Friedman argues that the change at hand is global in nature, fast in pace, and monumental in impact. We have moved from Globalization 1.0, which began in the fifteenth century with trade, to Globalization 2.0, which began in the nineteenth century with the industrial revolution, to today's Globalization 3.0, which is fully emerged in the current century. Version 3.0 is driven by education, technology, and an ever-shrinking world of deep interconnections. Moreover, today's transformation is a large-scale flattening, a leveling of the playing field: "It is now possible for more people than ever to collaborate and compete in real time with more people on more different kinds of work from more different corners of the planet and on a more equal footing than at any previous time in the history of the world. . . . When the world is flat, you can innovate without having to emigrate" (Friedman, 2005, p. 8). Friedman makes the case that with high-speed Internet, transparent trade, stable currencies, and political interdependencies, what happens in a faraway place—maybe halfway around the world—feels as though it is going on right next door. The flat world is a small world, after all.

Having served as the vice president for education and medical practice at SAS, the world's largest private software company, I saw this globalization firsthand. We had more than ten thousand employees in five hundred offices around the globe. The staff in our worldwide offices collaborate on everything from sales and marketing to research and development. R&D groups increasingly operate in a twenty-four-hour mode, with developers in Denmark, India, China, North Carolina, and Texas driving innovation and exchange around the clock. We are definitely not alone in using this strategy. Indeed, it is probably time for politicians and pundits to quit talking about companies outsourcing jobs. Rather, we should be talking about the internal and external *world sourcing* of jobs—leveraging diverse global assets in an elegant array of physical, fiscal, and human capital infrastructure.

Florida (2005) argues that the world has not become flat per se but deeply connected and "spiky." Put another way, he means that the flattening is not even; some countries, provinces, cities, and places are embracing change at a much faster pace. Their acceptance puts them out front in a very important race, the one for creative talent. As a result, their economic development fortunes are spiking up, while other communities are seeing theirs fall through the floor. Florida sees a shift from the agrarian age to the industrial age to the knowledge age, or what he calls the "creative age." Moving into the creative age means leveraging technology, talent, and tolerance to drive success. It also means fundamentally overhauling our societal infrastructures—such things as schools, public policy, and tax systems—to get there. However, some companies and communities are much better at this than others. People in some places *enjoy* the yeasty mixture of music, art, science, technology, and broader cultural acceptance because it gives rise to powerful economic and personal development. Other people in other places are not so ready, willing, or able to move in this direction.

Countries are moving quickly to take advantage of both the flattening and the spiking trends to draw talent and drive success. For example, Canada leverages its education system to bring in the best and brightest, and then it encourages them to immigrate. India and China are no longer talking about their strong math, science, and engineering programs as the main strategy to stop their brightest stars from studying and living abroad. They now want to build up their creative infrastructure, to support innovation and entrepreneurship as a means to keep their stars shining at home. Singapore's creativity campaign, called Thinking Schools, Learning Nation, is driven by education and aims to foster creativity and innovation.

All of this strategy is occurring in the context of a world awash in information. There are now literally billions upon billions of records, hundreds of millions of databases, an untold number of opportunities to learn more about companies, customers, and communities from the smallest of transactions and interactions on up. The connected, creative people that Friedman and Florida discuss have more information at their fingertips to tackle their challenges than ever before. Blackberrys, instant messaging, voicemail, online forms, and on-demand television conspire to keep us in a state of persistent partial attention. In a flat, spiky, talent-rich world, with always-on technology and increasing productivity demands, the stakes are getting higher every day.

There are broader and more significant changes as well. Here is one painful example: more than a billion people on our planet now live in extreme poverty, literally a cultural or conditional hiccup away from disaster (Sachs, 2005). Estimates are that twenty thousand people die every day of completely preventable diseases such as malaria and dysentery. Most poverty is found in Africa, Asia, and Latin America, but there are pockets elsewhere around the world, and this is a relatively new phenomenon. This disparity between the haves and have nots is concurrent with the industrial and creative revolutions about which we wax poetic. We may be raising the overall standard of living across the globe, but difficult humanitarian incidents are crippling countries at the bottom of the economic ladder.

Transcendent Skills to Consider

Given the scope of the change at hand—from flattening to spiking to starving—*what are the skills our students need?* What are the skills that will enable them to live well and free in this new world? I make the case for at least three: critical thinking, creativity, and courage. There is something about the confluence of these skills that holds the promise of making a difference for our students, communities, and countries. These are the skills I hear business and industry leaders calling for in meeting after meeting. These are skills that do not have a half-life; they can outfit our students for a better life in a globally connected world.

Critical Thinking. When I speak of critical thinking, I am talking about tough-minded tools for living and learning; the core thinking skills; the ability to take information, assess its sources, synthesize it, and analyze it. High-level analytics and decision making fit in here as well. Critical thinking is the ability to learn how to learn—to embrace continual learning. As Hoffer noted, "In times of drastic change, it is the learners who inherit the future. The learned usually find themselves equipped to live in a world that no longer exists" (1973, p. 32).

Critical thinking skills are important because of the impelling trend toward data-driven decisions. As Margaret Spellings (2005), the current U.S. Secretary of Education, notes: "In God we trust, all others bring data" (p. 1). With our world awash in the information streaming from almost every device and Website, critical thinking could not be more important. It is trite but true to say that we have more information at our fingertips than at any time in human history. However, if our students do not understand what the information means, which questions they are trying to answer, how to structure explorations or research, or how to apply the results, all of this raw material is meaningless; it is even dangerous. There is no such thing as data-driven decision making. It is *analysis-driven* decision making that really makes a difference. Because this is true, the combination of curiosity and capability is a must. Critical thinking is critical!

NEW DIRECTIONS FOR COMMUNITY COLLEGES • DOI: 10.1002/cc

In the January 2006 edition of the *Harvard Business Review on Decision Making,* Davenport (2006) referred to the advantage conferred by critical thinking skills as the power of competing on analytics. He studied a host of companies—from Amazon.com to Harrah's Casino to Marriott Hotels—that are leveraging analytical intelligence skills to make a major difference in how they compete and win in the marketplace. Davenport makes the case for analytical intelligence in pretty strong terms; he goes so far as to posit that analytical talent may be to the early 2000s what programming talent was to the late 1990s.

Some would argue that critical thinking skills have always been essential for science, technology, engineering, and math education. To reach the highest level, one needs to be able to analyze data, learn, and adapt. Thanks to daily processing of massive amounts of information in almost every industry, these skills are essential in virtually every profession. Remember: the world is flat, information is ubiquitous, and the ability to process that information to serve customers, improve products, or streamline operations may be the difference between success and failure for companies and communities.

Creativity. Critical thinking is not enough, however. All science and no art is dangerous; we have to embrace and inspire creativity as well. Florida (2005) argues that every person has a creative or artistic side. It is the unleashing of creativity along with intelligence that holds powerful promise. Unfortunately, if you study education you find that schools are notorious for whipping the creative spark out of their students—particularly underprivileged children (Kozol, 2006). In today's globally connected world, driven by the creative economy, the fact that many educators care more about rules and regulations than insights and innovations is more than a shame; it is insane.

At SAS, for example, we developed the Information Evolution Model (Davis, Miller, and Russell, 2006) to help organizations think about how they use information. The model has five levels, each more developmentally mature than the last. Level one is *operate,* where individuals who have specialized skills are the keepers and processors of information. Level two is *consolidate,* where departments or teams begin consolidating and sharing information to mine the past and report on the present. Level three is *integrate,* a bold step forward where the organization begins pulling its information together across the whole entity. Level four is *optimize,* where teams finally begin using predictive analytics and higher-level skills to discover the best ways to operate. However, it is level five, *innovate,* toward which we should strive. This is where we finally combine the science of analytics with the art of creativity. This is where the creative spark meets the fuel of information to transform operations. Once we have employees with the intelligence to understand, synthesize, and analyze their environment, coupled with the creativity to find new and novel solutions and strategies, we are almost there.

Many leading community colleges are taking creativity seriously. Paul Elsner, chancellor emeritus of the Maricopa Community Colleges in Arizona, talks about the importance of creative competition and allowing creative failures, and he models these behaviors in college leadership. Johnson County Community College in Kansas takes the culture of creativity so seriously that it raised money to open a museum of modern art, showcased two million dollars' worth of art around campus, and operates a stunning performing arts complex. Not surprisingly, this complex is directly connected to the college workforce development center. Similarly, Koning Willem I College, a community college in the Netherlands, opened a "Crealution Center" as part of their School for the Future. This center is dedicated to finding creative solutions (thus *crealution*) through group decision making based on modern brain research and creativity theory; it has become a mainstay of the surrounding business community.

Courage. The final skill, however, may be the hardest to acquire. We need a workforce with the courage to use the information, analysis, and creativity that is at their fingertips. The Information Evolution Model points to this challenge as it acknowledges that people, processes, and culture are the hardest to change. We can have the best technology, along with all the intellectual and creative capacity in the world; however, the hard work begins in boldly engaging difficult conversation, involving broad constituencies, and driving toward thoughtful solutions. A business leader can *know* that the business will fail without a hard turn in research and development, change in sales strategy, or a new approach to expenses. A hospital leader can *know* that a proposed solution may transform operations. However, if these leaders do not have the courage to take on the hard, sometimes painstaking work of engaging, involving, and transforming their organizations and communities, it is all for naught. *You* may even have the answer to world poverty, but fail to convince the right agencies and world powers and absolutely no one is saved.

I am not sure how we teach courage in our programs and degrees. Maybe it is best taught with case studies or mentoring. All I know is that our students will need courage if they want to make a difference. Make no mistake about it, courage is necessary to calm the caustic cynics and temper the true believers that always dominate the conversation surrounding change. Courage is necessary to champion new and novel solutions, to build a reasoned center of thoughtful critics and careful advocates to take up the banner of transformation. Courage is necessary to say there is a gorilla in the room when everyone else is blind to the danger.

Community college students know a good deal about courage. Milliron (2004) showed that many of our community college students exhibit it by overcoming their unique situational, personal, workplace, and financial challenges as they persist through our programs. We need to affirm their courage and help them continue to build on that boldness as they move on to their subsequent challenges.

NEW DIRECTIONS FOR COMMUNITY COLLEGES • DOI: 10.1002/cc

The Challenge

There is a *huge* gorilla in the room. Thankfully, the chorus of those who see it is getting louder. Now we need the courage to do something about it. Even though U.S. higher education is often pointed to as the cream of the crop, we have much work to do to meet the challenges of the global transformation at hand. Most of our schools and colleges are using an industrial factory model based on an agrarian calendar, to meet the needs of an information age. We are trapped in old models designed for very different times. Our arguments are too often about finding funding rather than fundamentally redesigning our colleges to impart internationally relevant and transcendent skills—particularly in workforce development.

We are not alone in this challenge. A host of innovators worldwide are challenging the status quo to transform their education systems. The Bologna Process in Europe is trying to open access and improve higher education transferability between European Union countries. The emergence of community colleges in China makes adult education more accessible and is driving the rise of the middle class. I saw an example last year of leaders using online fundraising to obtain money for rural schools in Brazil, which is now bringing resources to remote schools nestled deep in the rain forest. But progress is slow. For the most part, we are still facing tomorrow's world with yesterday's schools and colleges.

Finally, we need to take a deep breath and look at all of our policies, programs, and practices and ask hard questions about whether or not they are improving or expanding learning. As Florida (2005) argues, this education transformation must resemble the one we went through as we embraced the industrial revolution, and it must mirror the current economic transformation. Countries that wanted to compete in the industrial economy founded and funded secondary schools, tertiary schools, community colleges, and adult training resources. As the creative economy emerges, we need to ask what we should now found and fund?

The world is flat—or at least flatter than it used to be. Creativity is a commodity, with talent moving to inviting environments like moths to a flame. Moreover, difficult challenges face us in a great period of societal and economic transformation. It is our focused work today that will prepare or short-change the next generation of difference makers. We need to focus on preparing intelligent, creative, and courageous learners who are willing to face our challenges, build our economies, lead our companies, and transform our schools. Sachs (2005) even argues that with the right focus on education and action, we can end extreme poverty in our time. But to accomplish these big and bold projects, we have to harness the collective capacity of the next generation; we have to engage them and hold them to a higher standard. Gorilla or not, community colleges must take on this global challenge, help our students transcend their expectations, and prepare them for the change-filled road ahead. It is one of the highest callings of our time.

New Directions for Community Colleges • DOI: 10.1002/cc

References

Davenport, T. H. "Competing on Analytics." *Harvard Business Review,* 2006, 84(1), 98–107.

Davis, J., Miller, G., and Russell, A. *Information Revolution: Using the Information Evolution Model to Grow Your Business.* Hoboken, N.J.: Wiley, 2006.

Florida, R. *The Flight of the Creative Class: The New Global Competition for Talent.* New York: HarperCollins, 2005.

Friedman, T. *The World Is Flat: A Brief History of the Twenty-First Century.* New York: Farrar, Straus, and Giroux, 2005.

Hoffer, E. *Reflections on the Human Condition.* New York: HarperCollins, 1973.

Kozol, J. *The Shame of the Nation: The Restoration of Apartheid Schooling in America.* New York: Three Rivers Press, 2006.

Milliron, M. D. "The Courage to Learn." *League of Innovation Learning Abstracts,* 2004, 7(4), n.p.

Sachs, J. D. *The End of Poverty: Economic Possibilities for Our Time.* New York: Penguin Press, 2005.

Spellings, M. "Is America Really Serious About Educating Every Child?" *Education Writers Association 58th National Seminar.* Conference Proceedings, St. Petersburg, Fla., May 6, 2005 (http://www.ed.gov/news/speeches/2005/05/05062005.html; accessed Mar. 2, 2007).

MARK DAVID MILLIRON *is the Suanne Davis Roueche endowed fellow, senior lecturer, and director of the National Institute for Staff and Organizational Development (NISOD) in the College of Education at the University of Texas at Austin.*

NEW DIRECTIONS FOR COMMUNITY COLLEGES • DOI: 10.1002/cc

5

This chapter describes how globalism is changing the U.S. economy and the job market for community college students. Special emphasis is given to the changes required of technical and occupational programs in order to internationalize their curricula and the roles that administrative leadership and faculty play in the process of internationalization.

The Role of Globalization in Technical and Occupational Programs

Donald A. Dellow

As a former community college president and academic vice president, I have witnessed the ebb and flow of job markets in the communities in which I have lived. In the 1990s, the southern tier of New York experienced some of the most devastating industrial contractions in its history. This area had an abnormally high percentage of jobs in manufacturing (twice the state average in 1990), particularly in the computer and defense industries. The jobs seemed to disappear overnight; the unemployment rate increased rapidly and the area experienced a 6 percent outmigration of its populace. Jobs first moved to other areas of the United States, and then to other parts of the world. As unemployment increased, corporate training programs at the college became extremely popular. Health science programs increased enrollment while the oldest technical programs began to falter. My community was experiencing what Friedman (2005) notes are the effects of globalization in a very real and visible way. In recent months, I have had many discussions with community college colleagues around the country who are experiencing their own challenges with the global economy. Given the rapidly changing nature of the global economy, those of us in community colleges need to examine how globalization is affecting our occupational and technical programs, and develop strategies to prepare the workforce for life in this environment.

NEW DIRECTIONS FOR COMMUNITY COLLEGES, no. 138, Summer 2007 © 2007 Wiley Periodicals, Inc.
Published online in Wiley InterScience (www.interscience.wiley.com) • DOI: 10.1002/cc.280

How Is Globalization Affecting the U.S. Economy and Job Market?

To prepare our students for a global economy, we need to understand how globalization is changing the economy and job market. Coatsworth (2004) describes globalization as "what happens when the movement of people, goods, or ideas among countries and regions accelerates" (p. 38). Friedman metaphorically describes globalization as the shrinking of the globe, making travel, commerce, and communication less difficult. He goes on to describe how this shrinking is being driven by advances in computer technology, enhanced computer software integration capabilities, innovative low-cost telecommunications networks, and cheaper and more rapid transportation systems. One can think of these technological advances as the drivers of a global economy where borders become less important, making a new low-cost and highly skilled labor force more accessible to manufacturers, and generating new markets for the sale of products and services.

On a recent trip to China, I visited Suzhou Institute of Industrial Technology, an educational institution that was remarkably similar to an American community college. The institute was part of a large industrial park that contained dozens of major manufacturing companies and housing complexes for workers in those industries. One of the major programs at the college was computer numeric control (CNC) training. As part of the program, the institute gave students access to several CNC laboratories employing the newest technology. In one lab, there were twelve industry-standard CNC machines (with a retail price of about $40,000 each). When asked how many CNC operators were needed in the industrial complex, the answer was "many thousands and growing." Interestingly enough, students who graduate from the program earn $8,000 per year as a CNC operator. My point? In Suzhou, there is a postsecondary program producing CNC operators by the dozens, but who are paid a fraction of the salary they would receive in the United States. Companies are moving many of their U.S. operations to foreign countries where there is a well-educated workforce that can be hired at a fraction of the domestic cost.

The offshoring of jobs, especially in manufacturing and service industries (Blinder, 2006; Hagen, 2004; A. T. Kearney, 2004) has an impact on the labor market in every community college district, but it is not the only force affecting our domestic economy. The technological advancements noted earlier are also changing the domestic workplace by making workers more productive. Friedman notes that "most jobs are not lost to outsourcing to India or China—most lost jobs are outsourced to the past" (p. 278). The quest for better technology is increasingly fueled by the pressure of global competition to produce more for less.

Even the consequences of the impending skills gap—the scarcity of labor resulting from the retirement of the baby boomers—will be influenced by globalization. This phenomenon may affect the future labor market in

NEW DIRECTIONS FOR COMMUNITY COLLEGES • DOI: 10.1002/cc

two ways, one benefiting U.S. workers but the other hindering them. Certainly, there are fewer people to fill the jobs that baby boomers will be leaving, which opens the job market to younger workers. However, this labor scarcity may also encourage more businesses and industries to offshore jobs (A. T. Kearney, 2004).

Globalization is a topic that tends to be controversial. Friedman (2005) claims there is no controlling the global economy; the only strategy is to adjust and adapt. Others such as Stiglitz (2002) emphasize the inequities of globalization and suggest that leaders and world trade organizations take action to lessen the destructive impact globalization has on less-developed countries. This discussion is beyond the purview of this chapter, but it is important to note that community colleges must continue to prepare workers for the rapidly changing job market in their community. Consequently, the remainder of this chapter looks at what our community colleges must do to better prepare our students for a future where globalization continues to change the economy and community.

Community college educators must be keenly aware of globalization as they make decisions about programming. There are four major issues continuing to influence the labor prospects of community college students: How many American jobs, and which ones, will be lost to offshoring or outsourcing to the past? What new jobs will be created as a result of foreign investment in the United States, competitive pricing, and new technological advances? How will the skills gap change the job market? What skills will be needed for good jobs in the future?

It is safe to say that the answers to the first three questions will have an impact on our students, but it is difficult to predict the future considering that even economists cannot supply answers. Therefore the challenge for community colleges is to help students develop the knowledge and skills necessary for any eventuality in the global economy.

What Skills Are Needed for a Global Economy?

Several published research studies discuss the skills needed by community college students entering the workforce in a global economy. For example, some useful information has been compiled by research firms for university management schools. Bikson and Law (1994) presented data on how corporate leaders and business school faculty viewed the skills needed by workers for the global economy. These skills included strong domain knowledge; strong cognitive, social, and personal skills; prior work experience; and cross-cultural competence. More recently, Kedia and Daniel (2003) asked: "Do U.S. executives believe that international skills are important for the employees they hire? If so, what types of international knowledge are needed and at what level?" (p. 5). Usable surveys of 111 businesses in varying size (between five hundred and twenty thousand employees) and industry groups (manufacturing, service, retails, financial service, and telecommunications) were analyzed; the data offers specific guidance to which cross-cultural skills and international expertise community colleges must promote in workforce development programs.

Regardless of whether employees are involved in international manufacturing activities, negotiating and delivering professional services, or otherwise engaged in world commerce, awareness is growing of the importance of having more cross-cultural competence (Kedia and Daniel, 2003). In a global economy, more people will be dealing with colleagues and co-workers from around the world. The soft skills that have always been important for successful business practice become even more critical as business transactions take place between people from different countries and cultures. Several reports and studies (Hagen, 2004; A. T. Kearney, 2004; Bikson and Law, 1994) suggest that employees in the coming decades should have good interpersonal and communication skills; the ability to be part of an effective team; the ability to understand the global economy and the implications of globalization on world economies, the U.S. economy, and the local economy; the ability to use computer technology and productivity software; and the ability to find and use information on the Internet.

A Strategy for Responding to the Need for More Global Skills

It seems evident that community college educators have a major challenge to furnish students with the global skills necessary to compete in a changing economy. The strategy presented here is a guide to meeting this challenge.

Develop Global Awareness. This can be done by reading literature on globalization and discussing it with colleagues. Think about how globalization can change employment prospects in the field in which you are preparing students. Searching for articles that are written by international authors also helps develop new awareness. Finally, travel to countries that are emerging as the biggest competitors for jobs in your industry, and visit industries to see what is happening.

Survey Local Business, Industry, and Service Organizations. Survey your constituencies to determine which international and cross-cultural skills should be built into your programs. Obtaining this type of information from specific industry groups is necessary for planning curricular changes. The Kedia and Daniel survey instrument (2003) may be useful in formulating questions on specific international and cross-cultural skills.

Internationalize the Curriculum. Develop curricular and instructional activities that incorporate more international elements. Traditional programs must be more flexible if we want to help our students develop the skills needed for the new economy. Unfortunately, some existing occupational and technical programs are outdated and do not give students the skills they desperately need. If we as educators know that workplace skills are changing rapidly and choose to maintain fossilized program structures, proprietary institutions and corporate training programs will grow and our programs will continue to shrink. We must therefore challenge colleagues on curriculum committees to support a fast track for occupational and technical programs. This fast track will permit faculty to have greater flexibility in modifying the technical and occupational curriculum to meet the needs of industry.

There is also a need to focus on those activities that have an impact on the greatest number of students. It is unrealistic to think that a large number of part-time or full-time students are going to participate in study abroad programs. As Raby (2006) notes, the semesters our students spend with us may be the only higher education experience they will have. Consequently, it is critical to help students who do not travel abroad understand the need for greater global skills and create opportunities to develop those skills.

Faculty should also network with colleagues interested in internationalizing higher education. Seek out and attend conferences that focus on internationalizing higher education, and community colleges in particular. The National Association of Foreign Student Advisors (NAFSA) has a community college special interest group that focuses on internationalization. Community Colleges for International Development (CCID) also has a long history of focusing on international activities in the community college. By networking, institutions can learn from one another. There are plenty of examples of activities, projects, and curriculum development activities that have been developed for occupational and technical programs. Several excellent examples can be found in the Fund for the Improvement of Postsecondary Education's online grant database (http://fipse.aed.org/grantshow).

Finally, there is a need to use technology to create simulated or real opportunities to learn global skills. Raby (2006) cites a project that requires students to research the history, economy, and political climate of a country and then participate in computerized decision making about a worldwide problem, taking the perspective of the country they researched. Similarly, the International Business Practice Firm (IBPF) has been adopted by several colleges to engage students in a simulation of a real business venture with students in another country (Sepe and Kaufmann, 1998). In each case, faculty members have found ways to introduce the concept of the global economy while helping students develop greater global skill sets.

Curricular Transformation Will Be Challenging. As my colleague and I noted in a recent publication, "There will be a continuing conflict between the demand for short-term responsive programs and the emerging need for greater global competencies more typical of general education" (Dellow and Romano, 2006, p. 20). Most faculty members find it difficult to redesign coursework and curricula. The difficult question is always deciding which information and skills are most important for employees in today's global economy. If the program is short in length, it is more critical to make available as many global skills as possible.

Seek Institutional Support. This can be done by enlisting the support of colleagues and administrators. If the administration and your fellow faculty members are not supporting efforts to improve global skills, the process will be more difficult and time-consuming. New challenges need moral and spiritual support. It is also important to share your innovations and results. We community college educators must publish more to share our successes, failures, and dreams for the future. If we have good ideas and have made successful curriculum changes, we need to share them with our professional colleagues so they do not have to reinvent the wheel. The competition we are in today is not with our community college colleagues in the next county but with a world of very motivated, well-educated people who want to compete for the jobs we have in our communities.

Summary and Conclusions

The basic premise of this chapter has been that community colleges must internationalize their occupational and technical programs because globalization is changing local communities and job prospects for students. A general set of guidelines were discussed, which offer a framework for internationalizing campuses. The most critical elements of the framework revolve around the need for greater global awareness on campus and a major commitment to faculty development efforts to make changes in curricula and instructional techniques so as to foster a learning environment that is globally focused.

References

Bikson, T. K., and Law, S. A. *Global Preparedness and Human Resources: College and Corporate Responses.* Santa Monica, Calif.: RAND, 1994.

Blinder, A. S. "Offshoring: The Next Industrial Revolution." *Foreign Affairs,* 2006, 85(2), 113–128.

Coatsworth, J. H. "Globalization, Growth, and Welfare in History." In M. Suarez-Orozco and D. B. Qin-Hilliard (eds.), *Globalization: Culture and Education in the New Millennium.* Berkeley: University of California Press, 2004.

Dellow, D. A., and Romano, R. "Globalization, Offshoring, and the Community College." *Community College Journal,* Aug.–Sept. 2006, 18–23.

Friedman, T. *The World Is Flat: A Brief History of the Twenty-First Century.* New York: Farrar, Straus & Giroux, 2005.

Hagen, G. *Baseline Analysis of Offshoring in the Tampa Bay Region: Report Briefing and Policy Implications.* Tampa: Patel Center for Global Studies, University of South Florida, 2004.

A. T. Kearney. *The Future of Bay Area Jobs: The Impact of Offshoring and Other Key Trends.* San Francisco: A. T. Kearney Inc., 2004 (http://www.atkearney.com/shared_res/pdf/The_Future_of_Bay_Area_Jobs.pdf; accessed Mar. 3, 2007).

Kedia, B. L., and Daniel, S. "U.S. Business Needs for Employees with International Expertise." Paper presented at Needs for Global Challenges Conference, Durham, N.C., Jan. 2003.

Raby, R. L. "The International Negotiation Modules Project: Using Computer-Assisted Simulation to Enhance Teaching and Learning Strategies in the Community College." *IIE Networker,* Spring 2006, 51–53.

Sepe, T. D., and Kaufmann, M. "The Virtual Business Firm: Preparing Students for the Global Economy." *Community College Journal,* Oct.–Nov. 1998, 14–17.

Stiglitz, J. *Globalization and Its Discontents.* New York: Norton, 2002.

DONALD A. DELLOW is associate professor of adult, career, and higher education at the University of South Florida in Tampa.

This chapter profiles state and regional global education consortia, the successes they have enjoyed, and the challenges they face. It concludes with recommendations for strengthening these associations and ensuring their continued existence and effectiveness.

In Union There Is Strength: The Role of State Global Education Consortia in Expanding Community College Involvement in Global Education

Linda A. Korbel

In the late 1960s, a small number of community colleges gained prominence in the area of international education as they began to develop study abroad programs, faculty development opportunities, and international partnerships. These individual efforts led over time to the growth of national associations such as Community Colleges for International Development (CCID) and the American Council on International Intercultural Education (ACIIE), which began as the International Intercultural Consortium of the American Association of Community Colleges. These national groups had a fairly restricted membership base, consisting of larger community colleges with solid financial footing, and strong administrative or community support for initiatives that went beyond district borders. As with most associations, CCID and ACIIE derived common benefit from shared projects and from advocacy at the national level.

Unfortunately, given the costs of membership fees, travel to conferences, and participation in professional development opportunities, the majority of community colleges in a state or region were rarely able to fund participation in national associations. Thus over time collaborative groups were established in several states and regions to maximize the potential for program development by sharing the human and financial resources necessary to their

New Directions for Community Colleges, no. 138, Summer 2007 © 2007 Wiley Periodicals, Inc.
Published online in Wiley InterScience (www.interscience.wiley.com) • DOI: 10.1002/cc.281

work. These consortia began to develop shared activities, making learning opportunities more readily accessible to potential participants. It is often the case that one or two community colleges are dominant in a given state or region and have long-standing international programs that developed and sustained with local support. In some states, these institutions have taken a leadership role in working with their fellow community colleges to share opportunities and develop effective collaborations. For the purposes of this chapter, the term *consortium* designates a formal association of institutions in a state or region choosing to pool their human and financial resources to offer collaborative programs for all member institutions. This programming may include study abroad programs for students, professional development opportunities for faculty, study tours for the community, curriculum development in global education, and so forth. The obvious benefit is the opportunity to leverage staff time and budgets across multiple institutions, thereby offering programs and initiatives that few colleges can develop or sustain on their own.

In 1993, the ACIIE began a decade of collaboration with the Stanley Foundation. This collaboration set the stage for broad discussion of the role community colleges play in preparing a globally competent citizenry. The key to this effort was a series of thirty state and regional seminars, held between 1995 and 2000. For each event, every community college in a state or region was invited to send a team of five administrators, faculty, and trustees to spend twenty-four hours together, first listening to presentations about opportunities in global education and then meeting as an institutional team to formulate a plan of action to implement on their campuses. In nearly every seminar, establishment of a statewide consortium for international education became a component of these action plans. As a result of these seminars, hundreds of colleges initiated or enhanced global education initiatives on their own campuses. Collectively, ten global education consortia were established as a result of these seminars, joining those already created in the previous decade and a half. In 1998, ACIIE's leadership made a commitment to work with the state consortia to provide information, resources, and networking assistance. Since 2000, ACIIE has sponsored or cosponsored an annual meeting of consortium chairs to enable them to share the status of their organizations, the programs they have developed, and the challenges they face. Twenty-three associations have participated in one or more of the six annual meetings. Twelve consortia have formalized partner status in ACIIE.

The expansion of consortia efforts at the state and regional levels may very well have contributed to the growth in the field of international education between 1990 and 2000 (see Chapter One). Presidents and trustees who participated in consortia seminars lent encouragement to their faculty and academic administrators to develop international and intercultural programs. During this period, support from top leadership and statewide collaboration also facilitated establishment of international associations, even though the sustaining of such efforts fell primarily on the faculty (Table 6.1).

NEW DIRECTIONS FOR COMMUNITY COLLEGES • DOI: 10.1002/cc

Consortium Profiles

The profiles found in Table 6.1 clearly demonstrate the range of structure and activity of global education associations. In several states, informal gatherings of faculty with an interest in global education have taken place over time, ultimately leading to development of a more formal organization. Others were created between 1995 and 2000, following one of the seminars hosted by the Stanley Foundation and ACIIE. Some groups are nominally an association, a glimmer of hope in the eyes of a few committed individuals who have yet to bring their colleagues to the table in any consistent way. Other associations are a subset of their state-level governing board. Several of the associations include four-year colleges and universities, although most have only community college membership. Additionally, some associations have constitutions, by-laws, and officers, while others have virtually no structure at all. Some have a long track record, others are just getting started, and still others have ceased to function. Several associations have built-in support from the highest levels of governance in the state, and within their member institutions. Others are grassroots organizations, with a core group of interested faculty. Because community colleges have been willing to work together to furnish programs and services that might be too much for a single institution to coordinate, they have assumed their rightful place on the radar screens of funding agencies and support organizations, nationally and locally.

Consortia Success Stories

The common threads running through the consortia discussed in the preceding section offer an impressive depiction of what global education consortia have accomplished in two decades. They have sent thousands of community college students and faculty to study abroad. An even greater number of faculty and administrators have participated in locally organized seminars, workshops, courses, and conferences to enhance curriculum and program development. For example, the Illinois and West Virginia consortia have offered Fulbright group projects abroad. The Minnesota, Missouri, and Wisconsin consortia have received Title VI funding to develop international studies and programs. Similarly, the Virginia consortium has received National Security Education Program funding for travel to Vietnam. Consortia in Illinois, Minnesota, Texas, Ohio, Oklahoma, and Wisconsin have collaborated in hosting international scholars. Short-term, reciprocal faculty exchanges are offered in California, Illinois, Minnesota, Ohio, Virginia, and Wisconsin. Finally, the Illinois and Minnesota consortia have the authority to issue J-1 visas to enable member colleges to bring in foreign scholars and students. Unlike major universities, a single community college rarely brings in a sufficient number of international scholars each year to meet the State Department requirements for J-1 visa authorization. As a result access

Table 6.1. Active Global Education Consortia

Name	Membership and Funding	Programming
California Colleges for International Education; established in 1983; www.ccieworld.org	Seventy-two community colleges pay dues; volunteer board and officers	Represents community colleges in state-level associations of higher education: Southern California Council for International Studies, Northern California Advocates for Global Education, and California Council for Study Abroad
Florida Consortium for International Education; established in 1977; www.fcie.org	Eighteen two- and four-year institutions funded by local campus; volunteer representatives of member colleges	Umbrella organization for the Association of International Florida Linkage Institutes, the Florida Association of Community Colleges Global Commission, and the State University System of International Affairs Directors
Illinois Consortium for International Studies and Programs; established in 1986; http://web.sau.edu/studyabroad/icisp/AdministratorsPage.htm	Sixty-five two- and four-year institutions pay dues; volunteer board and officers, paid staff assistant	
Maryland Community College International Education Consortium; established in 2006	Sixteen community colleges, state support anticipated, volunteer representatives of member colleges	Recognition of the consortium by the Chief Academic Officers of Maryland
Massachusetts Council for International Education; established in 1991; www.fsc.edu/intled/macie.html	Twenty-nine public two- and four-year institutions; governing board with representatives from all colleges; local campus funding	
Midwest Institute for International and Intercultural Education; established in 1992; http://orgs.kvcc.edu/midwest	Ninety-two community colleges from several states pay dues; thirteen-member elected board	
Minnesota—EGL: Education for Global Learning; established in 1995; http://igs.cla.umn.edu/outreach/community%20colleges.htm	Thirteen community colleges and two universities pay dues; volunteer representatives of member colleges	

Missouri Consortium for Global Education; established in 1997; www.mocca.org/mcge	Seventeen community colleges pay dues; professional staff	
North Carolina Community College System; established in 1999; www.nccommunitycolleges.edu/global	Fifty-eight community colleges, system-funded	
North Texas Community and Junior College Consortium; established in 1988; www.unt.edu/ntcc	Twenty-nine community colleges and one university pay dues; consortium director on staff at a member college	
Ohio Community College Consortium for Global Education; established in 1999; http://www.cscc.edu/globaled	Twenty-three community colleges pay dues; volunteer chair	
Oklahoma Global Education Consortium; established in 1998; www.ogec.org	Fourteen community colleges pay dues; rotating volunteer chair, officers, and committee chairs	
Virginia Community College System International Education Peer Group; established in 2002	Twenty-seven community colleges, local campus funding, volunteer representatives of member colleges	
Washington State Community College Consortium for Study Abroad; established in 1999; http://washingtonstudyabroad.edcc.edu/whatis WCCCSA.htm	Fifteen community colleges pay dues; volunteer representatives of member colleges	
West Virginia Consortium for Faculty and Course Development in International Studies; established in 1980; www.polsci.wvu.edu/facdis	Twenty colleges and universities, state funding augmented by local college support	Summer institutes for public school teachers
Wisconsin Technical College System International Education Committee; established in 1994; www.wtcsglobaled.org	Sixteen technical colleges, system funding, volunteer officers and representatives of member colleges	Summer institute, World of International and Multicultural Work Skills

to these visas through a consortium or organization such as Community Colleges for International Development or the Fulbright program is often the only vehicle for bringing in international scholars.

The variety of programs, courses and curricula, participation levels, and creative partnerships demonstrate the range of possibilities that can be developed through global education consortiums. Yet all these success stories derive from only sixteen states. The absence of the remaining thirty-four does not diminish the outstanding global education initiatives undertaken by individual colleges in all fifty states. However, it does direct our attention to the difficulties that seem to work against successful collaboration.

Organizational Challenges to Global Education Consortiums

It is troubling to learn that several successful state consortia have become inactive in recent years, while two never moved beyond the concept stage. Once the Stanley Foundation's involvement and financial support for the consortiums ceased, associations in Colorado, Iowa, and South Carolina were unable to generate sufficient funding to sustain operations. Moreover, consortium leaders—current and past—have identified an array of challenges that their organizations face. Predictably, a steady and reliable source of funding is the challenge most frequently cited. Among the fourteen state associations responding to a recent request for information on the status of their organizations, all reported that the scope of their activity is defined primarily by the level of financial support. Consortia housed within the official state associations of community colleges generally enjoy a stabler financial outlook, given their access to infrastructure, which tends to be well funded by the institutions they serve. Those consortia that rely on separate membership dues often find that the smaller colleges have difficulty supporting such memberships and are less likely to be able to afford international programming of any kind. Thus integrating the global education component into existing state-level community college structures is one proven way of erecting a stable foundation of financial and staff support.

In addition to the cost of operations for state consortia, community college participation in global programming is further restricted by institutional budgetary concerns, scholarship support for student programs, release time for faculty, and liability concerns. The fiscal reality at individual colleges is magnified at the state level, where consortia may no longer be able to rely on the sustenance of member colleges to support consortial operations. The effectiveness of consortia is then limited, which decreases access to international programming that each member college formerly enjoyed.

Human resources are equally problematic. Many of the state associations have relied on the personal commitment and voluntary contributions of faculty and staff to organize and manage association business and shared programs. Of the associations profiled earlier in this chapter, only three currently have paid staff at the state level to support the association's operations. In some states, member colleges have financed involvement of their own faculty and staff to support the work of the consortium. For example, establishment of the Illinois Consortium for International Studies and Programs (ICISP) and subsequent growth to its current size and scope of activities were financed primarily by half a dozen member colleges that absorbed the cost of sending their faculty on site visits, supported travel to meetings, and offered release time to faculty who managed programs for ICISP. Unfortunately, many colleges permit no release time or other compensation for consortium work. The high rate of turnover among community college faculty and administrators due to retirement is another challenge; it has resulted in a shortage of leaders who support global education. Those pioneering crusaders, called to the mission of promulgating global education in the 1980s and 1990s, have left their posts. Sadly, it is much harder to find replacements who are willing do so much work for so little compensation and support. Creative approaches to compensation, incentives, and definition of work responsibilities will be needed in order to recruit new leaders.

It is also no surprise that the decades-old issue of justifying the rightful place of global education in the community college continues to surface. Ensuring a new generation of leaders who know and understand the critical importance of global education in community colleges, and who are committed to advancing its progress, is an ongoing challenge. As senior leaders in community college global education continue to retire, this challenge will only increase in scope. National associations such as the American Association of Community Colleges and the Association of Community College Trustees, along with state governing boards, local boards of trustees, and college administrations, must revisit their previous support for global education if they are to ensure that new leaders make it a priority. As well, state consortia can play a pivotal role in helping to educate new administrators and make the case for the importance of their active involvement in global initiatives.

Even when global education programs for students and faculty are in place, obtaining a sufficient level of interest and participation can be a problem. For example, the small number of community college students who study abroad is frequently attributed to the cost of such programs. But there are certainly other factors that limit participation. The paucity of community college study abroad participants may be a result of their family and work responsibilities, as well as their general lack of familiarity with international study. Community college educators face an uphill battle to make the case for global studies with their students, their communities, and their colleagues. As funding for financial aid decreases, it is a real challenge to engage low-income, minority, and first-generation college students in international programs. This concern has been voiced by national and state organizations and is being addressed by programs such as the Gilman Scholarship and the Abraham Lincoln Fellowship Programs, both of which target underrepresented populations for study abroad. However, policies established by funding agencies often restrict access by using eligibility requirements and program definitions that disadvantage community college students. For example, community college students are generally less able to participate in long-term programs, so they become ineligible for scholarships that require a full year or semester abroad. Consortia, as well as individuals, lose access to such programs if the federal program criteria are not sufficiently flexible to meet the needs of community college students.

Another impediment to effective consortial operations can be diversity among member institutions. Geographical distance, varying institutional type and size, community demographics and expectations, and an uneven level of institutional commitment all contribute to the difficulties associated with trying to offer an array of programs and services. If there are too many options, the already small pool of participants can become further diluted. A state consortium may develop a study abroad program in Mexico and successfully enroll thirty students each year, but this will not meet the interests of students who seek a program in Japan or Germany. Conversely, if programs are available in four or five locations, there may not be enough interest to sustain all of the program sites.

The need for training and professional development is another challenge. The most frequently discussed needs and challenges are curriculum development, faculty and staff development, resource development, creative partnerships development, low-cost-programs development, and management issues. These needs demonstrate the importance and the value of participation in international education conferences, seminars, Webcasts, and videoconferences, all of which regularly offer this type of professional development.

Recommendations

As is evidenced by the preponderance of consortial challenges over consortia success stories, community colleges must keep the importance of global education at the forefront of the national dialogue on higher education. Advocacy efforts must be redoubled and framed within the context of peace and international understanding, as well as the national interests of economic development and security. The pace and frequency of change in institutional leadership force us to resume our efforts to inform and convince those who will lead our community colleges. Here are recommendations that may help community colleges strengthen the delivery of global education.

Ensure Support from Senior Leaders. The commitment of the community college president and board of trustees is vital to the success of global education. They must recognize and value the need to educate their learners to thrive in a global society, incorporate it into their mission, and make available the institutional support to develop effective programs. Only then can leaders encourage their peers at other colleges to collaborate effectively to offer a comprehensive global education experience within their state. Furthermore, community college presidents in every state must be

NEW DIRECTIONS FOR COMMUNITY COLLEGES • DOI: 10.1002/cc

passionate advocates to their legislature and government leaders. The involvement of state community college oversight boards can facilitate the process of institutionalizing international education structures and furnish the resources necessary to support state associations.

Create Partnerships with Like-Minded Organizations. Organizations in the business of global education must continue to offer professional development and training for consortium leaders. Partnerships with the corporate world can be used to cultivate new international programming, scholarships, and internships, as well as give community college students access to international experiences. Considering the strong advantage given to collaborative partnerships in most grant criteria, community college consortia have to be more aggressive in joining forces with other organizations to seek the grant funding that already exists to support their initiatives. There is, indeed, strength—and opportunity—in union. State and regional global education consortia must seize those opportunities and forge ahead, to ensure that community college students take their rightful place as key members of our "globally and multiculturally competent citizenry" (ACIIE and Stanley Foundation, 1994, p. 1).

Reference

American Council on International Intercultural Education [ACIIE] and Stanley Foundation. *Building the Global Community: The Next Step.* Conference Proceedings, Warrenton, Va., Nov. 28–30, 1994.

LINDA A. KORBEL is dean of languages, humanities, and the arts at Oakton Community College and was executive director of the American Council on International Intercultural Education (ACIIE) from 1993 to 2006.

*This chapter explores how community colleges interna-
tionalize curricula by examining both on- and off-campus
strategies.*

Internationalizing the Curriculum: On- and Off-Campus Strategies

Rosalind Latiner Raby

The internationalization of the community college curriculum occurs through on-campus programmatic efforts and off-campus education abroad programs. As stated in Chapter One, growth in the field of international education is evident. However, it has not been institutionalized on many of our campuses. Despite two decades of efforts to internationalize the curriculum, this form of pedagogy remains at the periphery of most community colleges. This chapter explores strategies to internationalize the community college curriculum—to move international education from the margins to the core—by offering a context for future collegewide reforms. Examples from California Colleges for International Education (CCIE), a nonprofit consortium whose membership includes seventy-six California community colleges, are discussed.

Efforts to internationalize the community college curriculum infuse cross-cultural concepts, theories, and patterns of interrelationships into courses and academic programs. The international emphasis underscores the "need to understand a variety of perspectives (geographic, ethnic, cultural, gender, etc.) by acknowledging similarities, but also in a way that respects and protects differences among multi-country diversities" (Raby, 1999, pp. 3–4). On-campus internationalization strategies range from an individual faculty member's efforts to integrate independently gained knowledge into course content to systemic changes that result from purposeful collegewide reforms (Green and Siaya, 2005; Raby and Tarrow,

New Directions for Community Colleges, no. 138, Summer 2007 © 2007 Wiley Periodicals, Inc.
Published online in Wiley InterScience (www.interscience.wiley.com) • DOI: 10.1002/cc.282

1996). Off-campus internationalization strategies include education abroad, which embodies study abroad, work abroad, and international internships or volunteer programs. These two internationalization strategies are connected as travel entices faculty to revise curricula, which in turn inspires students to participate in internationally oriented programs and thereby gain international literacy skills.

Internationalizing Curricula: Establishing International Literacy Skills

A basic principle of internationalizing the curricula is development of a literacy that includes skills to perceive multiple perspectives, reconcile conflicting ideologies, and respect a relativity of differences. This literacy is a pragmatic tool that supports national security, prepares students for a globalized job market, encourages politically active citizens, and heightens problem-solving and listening skills. To achieve this literacy, curricula must include more than just awareness of basic cultural traits or geographic locals. It needs to establish a context for active learning in which "people begin to think in international and intercultural terms; where differences in response can be anticipated and understood merely as differences and not as right and wrong reactions; where one is constantly conscious of the different meanings and interpretations of the same words and expressions by people whose minds are conditioned by other languages" (Bhatia, 1985, p. 1). Pedagogically, it is critical to prepare community college students to live, work, and transact in our global world.

On-Campus Strategies for Internationalizing the Curriculum

Strategies to internationalize community college curricula range from individual acquisition of new knowledge to development of collegewide reform efforts. The likelihood of successful implementation depends on how the reform is introduced to each community college constituency. When reform comes from senior-level administrators, it is sometimes easier to modify college missions and policy documents, create curriculum committees, and establish a context for nonmonetary incentives such as release time and professional recognition. Those who control budgets can extend staff support for offices, approve faculty and staff travel, and encourage consortia or association memberships. Although top-down leadership is frequently encouraged in chapters throughout this volume, it does not always ensure success. Faculty support is also critical; they are the institutional actors who teach the internationalized curriculum, serve on international committees, and lead education abroad programs.

In creating collegewide reforms, it is essential to ensure that support for international education does not remain in the hands of a select few but rather is ingrained throughout the college. As is the case with any organization, programmatic efforts are affected when the faculty directors take a sabbatical, leave teaching for administration, move to another campus, or retire. To address such staffing changes and ensure program continuity, community colleges must constantly mentor new generations of leaders.

In addition to the aforementioned strategies, community college leaders can also employ six specific efforts to strengthen the curriculum; they are described here.

Diversify the Number of Modern Language Programs. The Committee for Economic Development (2006) has recently called for a dramatic increase in the number of Americans learning critical languages such as Arabic, Chinese, Russian, Hindi, and Farsi. Forty percent of the CCIE colleges offer at least one of these critical languages, and 25 percent offer at least three. In addition, most CCIE colleges offer between seven and twelve modern languages. It is not surprising that so many community colleges offer an array of language programs since these colleges serve their local populations, many of which are multiethnic. Although classes are offered, few colleges have a modern language program that offers multiple levels of every language. Moreover, many colleges fail to use language to support academic content. None of the CCIE colleges currently link language acquisition to graduation requirements, and most do not even connect language to other international programs at the college.

Target All Disciplines, Even Those That Need Extra Support. All community college disciplines (academic, technical, vocational, and occupational) are influenced by international relationships; *no* discipline is so provincial that it cannot be viewed from an international perspective. Courses with a comparative focus (literature, religion, government) or that address cross-border issues (cultural anthropology, cultural geography, ethnic studies, intercultural communications) are believed to be easily internationalized and are often targeted by faculty and administrators seeking to internationalize their college (King and Fersh, 1992). However, *ease* can be applied to all disciplines; faculty members simply need to reconceptualize the curriculum. For example, if child development faculty understand that not all children are raised the same way, it becomes easy to internationalize this discipline. Likewise, if a biology course includes a section on infectious diseases, the internationalization emerges from necessary inclusion of pandemics. All it takes is having college leaders understand that they need to embrace a philosophical shift that gives faculty the development opportunities to learn there is more than one way to view a particular subject.

Use the Experiences of International Students to Secure International Literacy. International students bring cross-border perspectives to class discussion. In addition, specific programs have been developed to take advantage of the learning opportunities that these students bring in. Among CCIE colleges, 60 percent use international students as guest speakers, 40 percent as culture tutors, 18 percent as study abroad orientation tutors, and 14 percent as language tutors. International students can become key resources for on-campus internationalization efforts, but college leaders must remember that not all international students possess the necessary skills to teach others, and international students' worldviews may not always represent their country's mainstream culture.

Infuse International Perspectives into Lesson Plans and Course Activities. Infusion takes place as faculty members add international ideas and themes into three to six lectures each term. Infusion is cost-efficient; it requires little more than faculty initiative and commitment. To infuse the curriculum, faculty can rely on life experiences, including international travel for business or pleasure, participation in internationally themed seminars, and discussion of internationalized components of the textbooks. Overt reform occurs when faculty members conduct purposeful research on international aspects of their class. In 2006, CCIE member colleges infused international content in 90 percent of cultural anthropology courses, 85 percent of cultural geography courses, 80 percent of ethnic studies courses, and 50 percent of intercultural communications courses. Examples of specifically infused courses are Ethnomathematics (Coast District); Asian Infusion (City College of San Francisco); Multicultural Health Beliefs (Hartnell College); and World Languages, Phrases, Foods, and Facts (Lake Tahoe College).

Though content infusion does not create drastic change, it is a safe way to introduce international components to the core curriculum. In an era of dwindling electives and greater focus on the core courses needed for a certificate or degree, the content infusion approach may be the most efficient way to internationalize the community college curriculum and ensure that all students are prepared to survive and thrive in a global economy.

Introduce New Course Content. In addition to infusing international education into existing courses, community college leaders can also make radical changes to existing classes or introduce new, specifically designed international courses. The International Negotiations Modules Project (INMP)—a computer-assisted simulation that places students in the role of the decision makers and negotiators on issues of global importance—is one such example. In INMP, the basic course content remains the same, but how the course is taught and its explicit international emphasis are unique. Students gain experience in understanding course content, how the content relates to their assigned country, and how countries and cultures perceive contemporary thematic and policy issues (Raby and Kaufman, 2000).

The addition of new courses sets a context for in-depth internationalization that the infusion approach lacks. New classes can be general (World Literature or Introduction to Global Studies), specific (Films of Latin America or Global Environmental Agriculture), or thematic (Spanish for Nursing or Chinese in Business). Unfortunately, compared to infusion fewer colleges add new courses. In 2006, 78 percent of colleges offered a course in non-European history, 72 percent offered international business, 70 percent offered non-European humanities, 52 percent offered international relations, and only 10 percent offered international or global studies. Some examples of new classes are Culture and International Business: Kiss, Bow, or Shake Hands (Santa Ana College); Introduction to Global Studies (Mission College); International Trade, Marketing, and Management (Long Beach City College); and International Politics (Santa Barbara City College). Although there are many benefits to adding new international classes, it is expensive, articulation with four-year universities is difficult, and campus curriculum committee approval is time-consuming.

Focus on Systemic Changes. Supporting change that permeates the entire college is the final on-campus strategy for internationalizing the curriculum. For example, a college can ensure that multiple courses are infused so that students take a range of internationalized courses that solidify their international literacy skills. The Asian infusion of fifteen City College of San Francisco courses is an example. Another type of systemic change is development of either a specific certificate or degree program (international studies) or the transition of an existing department (business becoming international business). In 2006, 20 percent of CCIE colleges offered a certificate or associate degree in international business. However, these programs vary widely. In 2005, Glendale Colleges had 25 students enrolled in their program, whereas Long Beach City College had 225, 90 percent of whom obtained employment immediately after receiving their degree. International business has established itself as a known program, but international and global studies has not. Only 4 percent of CCIE colleges currently offered a certificate or associate degree in international or global studies, and another 5 percent offer a degree in intercultural studies. One of the largest intercultural programs is at De Anza College, which graduated between ten and twenty students in 2005, 90 percent of whom transferred to a four-year university.

The ultimate systemic change is internationalizing general education graduation requirements. This includes a structured core of required internationalized classes, in addition to a selection of infused general education courses and electives. This optimal learning situation does not currently exist at any CCIE college. Sjoquist (1993) states that the general education curriculum ceases to be *general* if it is bound by a single culture. An internationalized core curriculum reflects a balance of cultural perspectives. Although focusing on systemic changes is clearly the best way to move international education from the periphery to the core of the community college curriculum, there are several challenges inherent in this approach. Procuring stakeholder support, securing faculty expertise, overcoming low student enrollment, and creating articulation agreements with feeder universities all serve as roadblocks.

In sum, intentional on-campus reforms occur through explicit and systematic changes in course content, academic programs, majors, certificate and associate degree programs, and ultimately general education requirements that holistically encompass the entire campus.

NEW DIRECTIONS FOR COMMUNITY COLLEGES • DOI: 10.1002/cc

Off-Campus Strategies for Internationalizing the Curriculum

Since 1967, community colleges have offered education abroad programs. According to the NAFSA Association of International Educators, education abroad is one of the more effective forms of internationalizing the curriculum because it embodies both content and physical presence in an international setting. For community college education abroad, classes involve the same requirements as those on campus but are modified to take advantage of the location in which they are offered. Community colleges offer single-subject, one- or two-week courses as well as summer and full-semester programs. Courses are credit-bearing and are in all academic, agricultural, occupational, technical, and vocational fields.

Numerous studies confirm the benefits of studying abroad for all students, especially those from underrepresented races, ethnicities, and income groups. Benefits include change in perception and attitude toward global relationships; increased empathy for politics and social service; significant growth in interpersonal skills, academic performance, language, and cultural proficiency; greater self-confidence; and reduction of cultural stereotypes (Raby and Sawadogo, 2005). There is no better environment than another culture to learn how to think about the world differently. In short, studying abroad is a life-altering experience.

Although community college education abroad continues to grow, only 0.01 percent of community college students study abroad annually (Institute for International Education, 2006). Moreover CCIE colleges, which lead the country in community college education abroad, send only thirty-eight hundred students abroad annually (0.06 percent of the total student population). The low participation rate begs the question: Why do so few students participate in education abroad?

Overcoming the barriers that prevent widespread student participation is crucial if colleges want to successfully internationalize their off-campus curriculum. However, defining these barriers has proven to be difficult. Lack of student interest, work and family obligations, and concerns about affordability are typically identified as the main reasons community college students do not study abroad. Interestingly enough, a recent study conducted by Coast Community College District, the Center for Global Education, and CCIE showed that these perceived barriers were not a significant factor in students' decisions on studying abroad (Raby and Rhodes, 2004). Although the seven hundred students surveyed agreed that financial barriers exist, 70 percent stated that finances alone would not deter them from studying abroad. Moreover, even though they acknowledged that family and work obligations make it difficult to take extended time off to study abroad, most surveyed indicated that they would be willing and able to participate in both short-term and long-term programs. According to the students surveyed, the primary barrier is institutional in nature; most community colleges do not offer education abroad opportunities or fail to adequately inform students about their programs. This finding is not surprising considering that more than two-thirds of CCIE colleges lack an office, full-time staff, or a college budget to support their education abroad (Raby and Rhodes, 2004).

In an effort to make education abroad more visible and accessible, CCIE—with funding from the International Foundation for Study Abroad—is helping member colleges introduce more semester-length programs. Several new programs have been developed or are in process that will have an impact for hundreds of new students. Some of these new programs are Ecotourism, Sustainability, and Peace Studies in Costa Rica (Butte College); Field-Based Ecology and Biology with Spanish Language in Peru (Lake Tahoe College); Marine Biology in Costa Rica (State Center District); French Immigrant Populations (Glendale College); and Indian Civilization (Ohlone College).

Other Off-Campus Education Abroad Programs. In addition to study abroad, there are other off-campus education abroad opportunities that internationalize the community college curriculum. The most popular are work abroad, international service, and foreign internship and volunteer programs. Although very few CCIE colleges offer professional internships at overseas businesses or organizations, 8 percent offer a program of an academic year abroad that includes an internship or work emphasis. Most of these programs are located in England. In addition, Santa Rosa Junior College in California offers a work, study, and internship program in the Australian wine region.

Steps Toward Reform

Despite a proclaimed commitment to internationalizing the community college curriculum among education leaders and policymakers, widespread implementation is rare. Fewer than one-sixth of CCIE colleges have established an international degree or certificate program, and none has internationalized general education requirements. Considering that 42 percent of CCIE colleges include international and global education in their mission statement, and that more than a dozen CCIE colleges have received federal grants to internationalize the curriculum, the dearth of progress is disturbing. There are several reasons international reform has not occurred on community college campuses. Unfortunately, these reasons are the same as those discussed more than a decade ago (Edwards and Tonkin, 1990; Raby, 2000; Green and Siaya, 2005). The next section discusses how community college leaders can surpass these barriers and move international programs from the periphery to the mainstream.

Enact Philosophical Change. Community college faculty and administrative leaders need to understand the benefits of internationalization. Moreover, they must incorporate internationalization in their college mission statement, strategic plans, and budgets; support it at every opportunity; and encourage others to do the same. A philosophical shift toward internationalization must occur if institutionalization of an international curriculum is to be realized. Furthermore, faculty and administrators must communicate and defend this shift to their peers, students, and the community at large.

Ensure a Budget for International Education. Without money, new international programs cannot be initiated or successfully maintained. As a result of budget shortfalls, some community colleges have cut international staff development activities, prohibited faculty from traveling abroad, and eliminated some study abroad programs. These actions do not help colleges prepare their students for success in a global marketplace. As such, college leaders must dedicate line items in the budget to ensure and protect funds for international programs and activities.

Support Staff Development. To effectively internationalize the curriculum, faculty must be involved in new research and creative application of international pedagogy and curricula. This requires time, enthusiasm, and collaboration with experts in the field. Administrative leadership must create and support opportunities for in-service training, conference attendance, and overseas professional travel. Stipends in the form of minigrants let the faculty know that their work in this area is being supported. Community college leaders must also honor faculty who infuse international knowledge in the classroom. However, such efforts take time and a considerable amount of staff development and administrative support.

Support Campuswide Internationalization Efforts. College leaders need to develop and fully support a centrally located office that furnishes information to students, faculty, and staff; and the office should collaborate with those who are involved in on-campus internationalization strategies and those who run study abroad programs. Community college leaders must also implement a systemic design to internationalize core courses, certificate and degree programs, and graduation requirements. Additionally, college leaders should support the long-range planning necessary for study abroad programs; adhere to known standards in the field; and develop a risk management program that addresses all legal, health, and safety issues. Finally, college administrators must develop broad-based coalitions with national and statewide consortia to help support and supply resources for education abroad programs.

Conclusion

For many students, the community college is the only opportunity to gain international literacy. Nonetheless, opportunities to study abroad or engage in an international curriculum are few. Even those colleges that offer internationalized programs rarely support them in a way that ensures maximum benefit. As shown in Chapter Two, 61 percent of U.S. community colleges still have a "low" level of internationalization (Green and Siaya, 2005), and only a handful of schools have institutionalized it as a component of their college.

NEW DIRECTIONS FOR COMMUNITY COLLEGES • DOI: 10.1002/cc

Community colleges must enact basic philosophical, economic, and institutional changes beginning with recognition that internationalization is a central element of a quality undergraduate education. Institutionalization of international reforms must include support from all college stakeholders as well as changes to specific courses and academic structures. Furthermore, international emphasis should be a defined criterion for faculty promotion, tenure, or release time. Although top-down leadership is important in many internationalization efforts, successful reform must also support bottom-up efforts that are based on faculty interest. Moreover, faculty buy-in must be the foundation for all internationalization efforts; it is imperative if international education is to survive through generations of college faculty, staff, and administrators.

It is critical to view the process of internationalizing the community college curriculum as both on- and off-campus ventures and to ensure collaboration between the two strategies. As this volume repeatedly argues, an internationalized curriculum is essential to promote international competency among community college students, faculty, administrators, and staff. Knowledge and understanding of other societies, histories, geographic environments, values, institutions, and cultural traditions is essential for comprehending the complex, interconnected matrix of our world. Understanding how culture shapes our own policies and agendas—as well as those in other parts of the world—has a direct relationship with our capacity to make personal decisions on complex international issues. Indeed, investment in internationalizing the community college curriculum is an investment in prevention.

References

Bhatia, V. N. "The Use of the Curriculum in Internationalizing the University." *Journal of the AIERA,* 1985, 5(1), 1–10.

Committee for Economic Development. *Education for Global Leadership: The Importance of International Studies and Foreign Language Education for U.S. Economic and National Security.* Washington, D.C.: Committee for Economic Development, 2006 (http://www.ced.org/docs/report/report_foreignlanguages.pdf; accessed Mar. 1, 2007).

Edwards, J., and Tonkin, H. "Internationalizing the Community College; Strategies for the Classroom." In R. Greenfield (ed.), *Developing International Education Programs.* New Directions for Community Colleges, no. 70. San Francisco: Jossey-Bass, 1990.

Green, M., and Siaya, L. *Measuring Internationalization at Community Colleges.* Washington, D.C.: American Council on Education, 2005.

Institute for International Education. *Open Doors: Report on International Educational Exchange.* New York: Institute for International Education, 2006 (http://opendoors.iienetwork.org/; accessed Mar. 1, 2007).

King, M. C., and Fersh, S. H. *Integrating the International and Intercultural Dimension in the Community College.* Washington, D.C.: Association of Community College Trustees and Community Colleges for International Development, 1992.

NAFSA, Association of International Educators. *Internationalizing the Curriculum and Campus Network.* Washington, D.C.: NAFSA, Association of International Educators, 2006 (http://www.nafsa.org/knowledge_community_network.sec/teaching_learning_and/internationalizing_the_3; accessed Mar. 3, 2007).

Raby, R. L. *Looking to the Future: Report on International and Global Education in California Community Colleges.* Sacramento: Chancellor's Office of the California Community Colleges, 1999.

Raby, R. L. *Internationalizing the Community College Curriculum: Theoretical and Pragmatic Discourses.* New York: NAFSA Association of International Educators, 2000.

Raby, R. L., and Kaufman, J. "Navigating the Digital Divide: Using Technology to Internationalize Community College Curricula." *International Journal of Educational Policy Research and Practice,* 2000, *1*(3), 389–405.

Raby, R. L., and Rhodes, G. *Barriers to Student Participation in California Community Colleges.* Sacramento: Chancellor's Office of the California Community Colleges, 2004 (http://coastline.cccd.edu/page.asp?LinkID=635#section3; accessed Mar. 3, 2007).

Raby, R. L., and Sawadogo, G. "Education Abroad and Community Colleges." In J. L. Brockington, W. W. Hoffa, and P. C. Martin (eds.), *NAFSA's Guide to Education Abroad for Advisers and Administrators* (3rd ed.). Washington, D.C.: NAFSA, Association of International Educators, 2005.

Raby, R. L., and Tarrow, N. (eds.). *Dimensions of the Community College: International, Intercultural, and Multicultural Perspectives.* New York: Garland, 1996.

Sjoquist, D. P. "Globalizing General Education: Changing World, Changing Needs." In N. A. Raisman (ed.), *Directing General Education Outcomes.* New Directions for Community Colleges, no. 81. San Francisco: Jossey-Bass, 1993.

ROSALIND LATINER RABY is director of the California Colleges for International Education and senior lecturer in the College of Education at California State University, Northridge.

NEW DIRECTIONS FOR COMMUNITY COLLEGES • DOI: 10.1002/cc

This chapter explores the Education for Global Learning (EGL) consortium's efforts to assess intercultural competence as an outcome of study abroad. The chapter concludes with lessons learned and next steps in EGL's international education journey.

Expanding the Vision of International Education: Collaboration, Assessment, and Intercultural Development

Holly A. Emert, Diane L. Pearson

Educational systems have a responsibility to give students the knowledge and skills necessary to become productive members of society. In the twenty-first century, this responsibility means preparing students to be globally literate so that they can "recognize global interdependence, be capable of working in various environments, and accept responsibility for world citizenship" (Spaulding, Mauch, and Lin, 2001, p. 190). To foster global literacy in students, community colleges need to create intercultural learning opportunities that promote development of culturally appropriate knowledge, skills, and attitudes in and outside the classroom (Martin and Nakayama, 2004). International education efforts are an important way in which these institutions can promote this intercultural competence in students.

After briefly examining the mandate for international education, internationalization, and intercultural competence, this chapter describes Education for Global Learning: A Consortium of Minnesota State Colleges and Universities (EGL), emphasizing its assessment of intercultural competence as an outcome of study abroad. EGL is a collaboration of faculty at thirteen community colleges and two state universities in Minnesota who work together to internationalize their campuses. The chapter concludes with a discussion of the lessons learned by EGL and its next steps in the internationalization journey.

NEW DIRECTIONS FOR COMMUNITY COLLEGES, no. 138, Summer 2007 © 2007 Wiley Periodicals, Inc.
Published online in Wiley InterScience (www.interscience.wiley.com) • DOI: 10.1002/cc.283

The Mandate for International Education, Internationalization, and Intercultural Competence

International education comprises educational efforts that infuse globally oriented content, perspectives, and experiences into all levels of education as a means to increase awareness and understanding of the diverse world in which we live. At the postsecondary education level, this change movement is termed *internationalization* and can occur both within a domestic setting, through curricular integration of culturally pluralistic content into course content, and abroad, through provision of study abroad programs.

At its core, internationalization is "the process of integrating an international, intercultural or global dimension into the purpose, functions, or delivery of postsecondary education" (Knight, 2003, p. 2). It is "an ongoing, future-oriented, multidimensional, interdisciplinary, leadership-driven vision that involves many stakeholders working to change the internal dynamics of an institution to respond and adapt appropriately to an increasingly diverse, globally focused, ever-changing external environment" (Ellingboe, 1996, p. 199). One of the desired outcomes of internationalization is cultivation of an intercultural mind-set and skill set in students. Intercultural competence is a key goal of internationalization because it indicates awareness and understanding of culturally diverse others and situations, as well as the presence of behaviors that promote productive and effective communication among and across cultures.

Given the global environment of the twenty-first century, there is a heightened need for community colleges to foster opportunities to students that promote intercultural competence, irrespective of whether these students travel outside their home city, region, or country (Levin, 2002; Otten, 2003; Raby, 1996). Of particular note are increasing demographic changes within the United States that make international and intercultural competence essential for our students. In the Minneapolis–St. Paul metropolitan area and throughout the state of Minnesota, the community college community is welcoming an increasing number of students who emigrate from countries in Latin America, East and West Africa, and Southeast Asia.

However, community college campuses vary greatly in terms of resources and support for the work of internationalization (Siaya and Hayward, 2003). This local variability exists among EGL member institutions; it was this inconsistency of resources and support that brought these colleges together to collaborate and support one another in promoting their internationalization efforts.

The Education for Global Learning Consortium

The mission of Education for Global Learning: A Consortium of Minnesota State Colleges and Universities (EGL) is "to create, promote, support, and facilitate a range of international education learning opportunities and expe-

NEW DIRECTIONS FOR COMMUNITY COLLEGES • DOI: 10.1002/cc

riences for students, faculty, staff, and administration on the local campus, throughout the state, and around the world" (Education for Global Learning, 2006, p. 1). EGL leadership comes from members of the EGL board; representatives include faculty campus leaders, international student counselors, and academic deans from member campuses. Representatives from all member colleges participate in monthly meetings to share information and discuss their internationalization successes and challenges.

Since its founding in 1995, EGL has accomplished many of its internationalization goals. In the last decade, it has coordinated the sharing of resources, ideas, and projects among member campuses; furnished resources to invite an increasing number of international scholars to campuses; organized annual global education conferences; lent support for local campus programs; and developed study abroad opportunities for students and faculty (Education for Global Learning, 2006). EGL has fulfilled these goals despite encountering a number of challenges, such as state-level reorganization of postsecondary institutional structures and lack of consistent funding and support from local and system-level administrators and faculty. By working together, EGL's members enhanced collective efforts to implement internationalization change strategies at the local and system levels.

Study Abroad and Intercultural Competence

Study abroad is a significant component of the EGL internationalization strategy, enhancing international programming and promoting development of students' intercultural competence. But what is intercultural competence? Many authors group components of intercultural competence into the three categories of knowledge, attitudes, and behaviors or skills. The knowledge category includes the cognitive information that an individual takes into an intercultural situation, for example, knowledge of self. The attitudes category includes the emotions and intentions of communication, such as empathy. Behaviors and skills refer to the actions that indicate success in an intercultural encounter; the ability to complete a task is an example. Although consensus on a definition of intercultural competence is hard to find, it can be summarized as "the ability to communicate effectively and appropriately in intercultural situations based on one's intercultural knowledge, skills, and attitudes" (Deardorff, 2006, p. 247). For students to successfully interact with culturally diverse individuals, they need to understand and have the capacity to respond appropriately to culture-based cues and situations. One powerful way to purvey these learning opportunities to students is through participation in study abroad programs.

There is a rich literature on study abroad outcomes and on how taking part in experiences abroad can increase intercultural awareness and skills. Research indicates that sojourners often increase their perspective-taking skills (Steglitz, 1993), improve their language learning abilities and proficiency (Freed, 1995; Paige, Jacobs-Cassuto, Yershova, and DeJaeghere, 2003), and acquire cross-cultural knowledge and culture learning skills (Carlsson-Paige and Lantiere, 2005) as a result of their study abroad experience.

In the EGL consortium there are two, semester-long study abroad programs located in Costa Rica and at Oxford University in England. These programs are run collaboratively by EGL member institutions; EGL faculty members teach in these programs. Over the past decade, thirty-nine community college faculty and 450 students from eleven community college campuses have participated in these study abroad programs.

EGL and the Need for Assessment

Although many institutions of higher education are challenged to create curricula and experiences that nurture global literacy and intercultural competence, community colleges face unique challenges. Study abroad is a more difficult internationalization project to launch and sustain—let alone expand—in the community college environment (Siaya and Hayward, 2003). Study abroad programming requires substantial institutional resources and infrastructure, not to mention adequate student enrollment. Moreover, study abroad has traditionally not been viewed by administrators, faculty, and the public at large as vital to the education of community college students.

The challenge for the EGL consortium, therefore, has been to demonstrate why study abroad is relevant and appropriate, if not essential, for students. One way to extend legitimacy to study abroad is to clearly demonstrate the educational outcomes it produces. In the present era of accountability-driven assessment of learning outcomes, it has been important for the EGL leadership to emphasize assessment as a key aspect of its study abroad programming, for several reasons. First, the assessment of student learning that results from study abroad would yield data that EGL could use to improve its study abroad programs. Second, assessment results could enhance awareness of the educational value of study abroad with the aim of increasing administrative support for expanded EGL study abroad opportunities. To quantify the effectiveness of its study abroad programs and show how it promotes acquisition of intercultural competence in students, EGL instituted use of the Intercultural Development Inventory (Hammer and Bennett, 1998) as a required part of its study abroad programs beginning in 2003.

Implementation of the Intercultural Development Inventory

The Intercultural Development Inventory (IDI) is a fifty-item instrument that measures an individual's worldview toward cultural difference. In addition to the fifty items, there are demographic questions related to gender, age, amount of previous experience living in another culture, completed level of education, and global region of residence during the first eighteen years

NEW DIRECTIONS FOR COMMUNITY COLLEGES • DOI: 10.1002/cc

of life. The theoretical basis of the IDI is the Developmental Model of Intercultural Sensitivity (DMIS), which consists of six stages representing a continuum of increasingly sophisticated intercultural sensitivity, from ethnocentric to ethno-relative orientations (Bennett, 1993). An ethnocentric worldview represents an avoidance or disavowal of cultural difference in some form. Individuals with an ethno-relative worldview, on the other hand, experience their own culture and others in relation to each other and placed within a given context. Within the ethnocentric and ethno-relative stages of the DMIS, there exist three substages. The first three stages—denial, defense, and minimization—are considered ethnocentric in that they represent a primarily monocultural view of cultural difference, with one's own cultural worldview as the basis for understanding others owing to limited experience with culturally diverse others. The second three stages—acceptance, adaptation, and integration—are considered ethno-relative because individuals in these stages have a plurality of cultural viewpoints born in substantive experience with members of other cultural groups such that their own cultural worldview is but one of many possible realities. In sum, the DMIS posits that "as one's experience of cultural difference becomes more sophisticated, one's competence in intercultural relations potentially increases" (Hammer, Bennett, and Wiseman, 2003, p. 423). It is the ability to interpret cultural difference on the basis of subjective personal experience with cultural diversity that enables intercultural competence to develop.

The IDI was chosen as EGL's primary assessment tool for several reasons. First, a theoretically based measure was sought to assess the impact of the study abroad experience on the intercultural sensitivity of students, and the DMIS is a theoretically grounded framework. Second, the IDI has undergone extensive psychometric testing and is a reliable and valid measure (Hammer, Bennett, and Wiseman, 2003; Paige, Jacobs-Cassuto, Yershova, and DeJaeghere, 2003). Third, there is an established research literature base illustrating its use (Paige, 2003). On the basis of its grounding in theory, its empirical reliability and validity, and the fit with EGL assessment goals, the IDI was deemed the best choice to measure students' intercultural sensitivity.

Participants. Eighty-eight community college students (twenty-seven males, sixty-one females) enrolled in EGL's Costa Rica program between 2004 and 2006, and forty-three students (eighteen males, twenty-five females) enrolled in the Oxford University program between 2003 and 2005; all students participated in the IDI-based program evaluations. Sixty-two percent of participants were between the ages of eighteen and twenty-one, while 31 percent were between twenty-two and thirty. Examined as a combined group, 91 percent of the students spent their formative years in North America, while other students listed Eastern Europe, Western Europe, South America, Central America, and the Middle East as region of origin. Relative to living experience in another culture, 38 percent of these students indicated they had never done so, 40 percent had spent less than three months in another culture, and 20 percent of students had spent from three months to ten years living elsewhere. This brief review of participants' demographic data shows wide variability in student background and experience.

Procedures. Administration of the IDI took place as part of each study abroad program's mandatory predeparture orientation session. As part of the session, a certified IDI administrator presented students with the rationale for use of the IDI, followed by a discussion of culture and cultural self-awareness in preparation for completing the instrument; students were allowed to opt out of taking the IDI. The IDI took students between twenty and thirty minutes to complete. EGL students were not required to give their names initially, because the goal of using the IDI was for program evaluation, not assessment of individual intercultural learning.

Scoring. Using the available IDI software, scoring of the IDI produces an overall developmental score and several subscale scores. The developmental score has a range of 55–145 points with a mean of 100. The subscales and their point ranges are denial-defense and reversal, 55–84; minimization, 85–114; and acceptance-adaptation, 115–145.

Results and Discussion. IDI results are reported in the aggregate, analyzed by program destination and program year and as a combined group over time for each study abroad destination. Overall, the IDI results indicated growth in the intercultural competence of all groups pretest to posttest, regardless of program destination or year.

The IDI pretest scores for all groups fell in the minimization range of 85–114, as did the posttest scores. For the Costa Rica group, pretest to posttest scores increased from 91.13 to 93.84 in 2004, from 91.47 to 94.00 in 2005, and from 89.53 to 92.12 in 2006. For the Oxford study abroad groups, pretest to posttest scores increased from 103.18 to 104.66 in 2003 and from 95.69 to 97.87 in 2005. The changes, albeit small, indicate that students in all groups reduced their ethnocentric tendencies. It is not unusual that student scores progressed within—but did not move past—the stage in which they began. This is due, in part, to the developmental nature of intercultural competence, where significant experience with cultural difference, often over an extended period of time, is typically needed before a substantial shift in worldview can occur.

Of interest is the finding that students who studied abroad in Oxford had higher pretest and posttest developmental scores each year than students who studied in Costa Rica. Possible explanations for this finding include differences in program requirements, course content, and student characteristics. The IDI data collected to date cannot reveal exactly why this is the case; further collection and analysis of data related to student expectations and academic background may illustrate why there seems to be differences between groups by program destination.

The growth in scores in the minimization range indicates that students' experiences abroad fostered greater awareness of culturally diverse others in such a way that students could better differentiate cultural categories. Despite the positive growth in worldview, scores in the minimization stage indicate that individuals tended to highlight cultural similarities rather than engaging with culturally diverse individuals from the perspective of the culturally different group. This tendency to interpret the experience of other cultures through one's own cultural lens occurs primarily because individuals have not had enough experience with other cultural viewpoints to comprehend and interpret the world through another cultural perspective (Bennett, 1993). The need to gain substantive experience interacting with culturally diverse individuals as a means to broaden one's worldview is why study abroad is of high value for students.

Lessons Learned and Next Steps

EGL has learned several lessons as a result of its use of the IDI for study abroad program evaluation. By using an empirical measure of intercultural competence, EGL has increased the credibility and legitimacy of its study abroad programs as an integral part of the internationalization process. Second, the IDI findings have shown that EGL study abroad programs increased the intercultural competence of students. However, because students were not initially required to give their name on the IDI, EGL was not able to match individual pretest and posttests, which inhibited statistical analysis. The ability to conduct more rigorous analysis of IDI and other data is important so that EGL can more clearly understand the aspects of EGL study abroad programs that contribute to student learning. Despite this hindrance, the IDI has revealed many useful insights about EGL students, such as the diversity of students by age and prior experience with other cultures. Community colleges that are interested in implementing assessment measures such as the IDI should consider issues such as the need to secure financial resources for the costs of the instrument and for the services of a certified IDI consultant. College leaders should also obtain administrative and faculty buy-in concerning the importance of study abroad program assessment.

From their positive experience assessing the impact of participation in EGL study abroad programs on the intercultural competence of students, EGL leaders are currently implementing several steps to promote development of intercultural competence for students and faculty in the future. These steps include implementation of faculty development sessions on intercultural knowledge and processes to help them develop curricula and assessment activities to improve student learning, inclusion of intercultural communication and other cultural adjustment skill training as part of predeparture orientations, development and delivery of curricular and other programming for use while abroad to help students better understand and reflect on the intercultural learning that is taking place, and provision of reentry programming for students to help them reflect on and ultimately apply the intercultural learning that occurred while abroad.

Conclusion

This chapter has explored how the Education for Global Learning consortium has furthered its internationalization efforts through assessment of intercultural competence as an outcome of study abroad. Through its experience delivering programs and working with faculty and students, the EGL leadership decided they needed to assess their programs more rigorously; the Intercultural Development Inventory was implemented as a step toward that goal. Its use has shown that EGL study abroad programs positively affect student learning and development of students' intercultural competence. Given the continued efforts of EGL member faculty and staff in their work to mentor the next generation of faculty leaders, as well as continued demand by students for international and intercultural programming and curricular offerings, EGL will continue to improve on and expand its international education work far into the future.

References

Bennett, M. J. "Towards Ethnorelativism: A Developmental Model of Intercultural Sensitivity." In R. M. Paige (ed.), *Education for the Intercultural Experience.* Yarmouth, Maine: Intercultural Press, 1993.

Carlsson-Paige, N., and Lantiere, L. "A Changing Vision of Education." In N. Noddings (eds.), *Educating Citizens for Global Awareness.* New York: Teachers College Press, 2005.

Deardorff, D. K. "Identification and Assessment of Intercultural Competence as a Student Outcome of Internationalization." *Journal of Studies in International Education,* 2006, *10*(3), 241–266.

Education for Global Learning. *Education for Global Learning Mission Statement.* Minneapolis: Education for Global Learning, 2006.

Ellingboe, B. J. "Divisional Strategies on Internationalizing Curriculum: A Comparative Five-College Case Study of Deans' and Faculty Perspectives at the University of Minnesota." Unpublished master's thesis, Department of Educational Policy and Administration, University of Minnesota, 1996.

Freed, B. F. (ed.). *Second Language Acquisition in a Study Abroad Context.* Philadelphia: John Benjamins, 1995.

Hammer, M. R., and Bennett, M. J. *The Intercultural Development Inventory Manual.* Portland, Ore.: Intercultural Communication Institute, 1998.

Hammer, M. R., Bennett, M. J., and Wiseman, R. "Measuring Intercultural Sensitivity: The Intercultural Development Inventory." *International Journal of Intercultural Relations,* 2003, *27*(4), 421–443.

Knight, J. "Updated Internationalization Definition." *International Higher Education,* 2003, *33,* 2–3.

Levin, J. S. "Global Culture and the Community College." *Community College Journal of Research and Practice,* 2002, *26,* 121–145.

Martin, J. N., and Nakayama, T. K. *Intercultural Communication in Contexts.* New York: McGraw-Hill, 2004.

Otten, M. "Intercultural Learning and Diversity in Higher Education." *Journal of Studies in International Education,* 2003, *7*(1), 12–26.

Paige, R. M. "Intercultural Development." *International Journal of Intercultural Relations,* 2003, *27*(4), 421–443.

Paige, R. M., Jacobs-Cassuto, M., Yershova, Y., and DeJaeghere, J. "Assessing Intercultural Sensitivity: An Empirical Analysis of the Hammer and Bennett Intercultural Development Inventory." *International Journal of Intercultural Relations,* 2003, 27(4), 467–486.

Raby, R. L. "Internationalizing the Curriculum." In R. L. Raby and N. Tarrow (eds.), *Dimensions of the Community College: International, Intercultural, and Multicultural Perspectives.* New York: Garland, 1996.

Siaya, L., and Hayward, F. M. *Mapping Internationalization on U.S. Campuses.* Washington, D.C.: American Council on Education, 2003.

Spaulding, S., Mauch, J., and Lin, L. "The Internationalization of Higher Education: Policy and Program Issues." In P. O'Meara, H. D. Mehlinger, and R. M. Newman (eds.), *Changing Perspectives in International Education.* Bloomington: Indiana University Press, 2001.

Steglitz, I. E. "Intercultural Perspective-Taking: The Impact of Study Abroad." Unpublished doctoral dissertation, University of Minnesota, Twin Cities, 1993.

HOLLY A. EMERT *recently earned her Ph.D. in comparative and international development education from the University of Minnesota and has worked with the EGL program leadership since 2003 to assess their internationalization efforts.*

DIANE L. PEARSON *is on the social science faculty at Minneapolis Community and Technical College, the founder and chair of EGL, and an executive committee member of the American Council for International and Intercultural Education.*

*This chapter profiles international faculty in U.S.
community colleges, compares them to noninternational
faculty, and calls for greater emphasis on this often-
overlooked group in future policies and research.*

International Faculty in U.S. Community Colleges

Ryan Wells

Despite claims that community colleges are successfully engaging international education, the fact remains that the "majority of community colleges have not made a stated commitment to internationalization" (Siaya and Hayward, 2003, p. 31). When institutions do make efforts to implement comprehensive internationalization, they often extend study abroad, internationalize curricular content, create international events on campus, and recruit international students (Chase and Mahoney, 1996; Knight, 2004). Although such efforts are worthwhile, another aspect of internationalization is often overlooked: recruitment and retention of international faculty members.

For the purposes of this chapter, the term *international faculty* refers to all faculty members other than American-born U.S. citizens. This view consciously diverts from the narrow view of international faculty members as visiting, short-term, foreign faculty. The definition has the advantage of including faculty members who may be naturalized citizens or permanent residents but who nonetheless have perspectives, attitudes, and values that are likely to be internationally influenced. This categorization scheme is not perfect, however. The definition used in this chapter may include U.S. citizens who were naturalized at a young age and who identify more as American than as any other nationality. It also excludes American-born faculty who may have spent significant time abroad, some of whom may be significantly international. Data do not exist to study these specific cohorts in any

NEW DIRECTIONS FOR COMMUNITY COLLEGES, no. 138, Summer 2007 © 2007 Wiley Periodicals, Inc.
Published online in Wiley InterScience (www.interscience.wiley.com) • DOI: 10.1002/cc.284

meaningful way. Nevertheless, compared to noninternational faculty members, international faculty are likely to bring a range of diverse, international perspectives to the campuses where they work, making this study a worthwhile first step toward a more comprehensive research effort.

This study is based on three premises. First, international education is a valuable endeavor for community colleges because it yields benefits for student learning and development (Biddle, 2002; Knight, 2004). Second, international faculty members who come with valuable international experience and expertise are an important part of comprehensive internationalization. Third, attention to an internationalized faculty as a means of internationalization has not been well promoted, as evidenced by the fact that fewer than 3 percent of community colleges have policies that take international experience into account for promotion or tenure decisions (Siaya and Hayward, 2003). This chapter broadens our understanding of international faculty in U.S. community colleges and gives administrators a deeper understanding of the professional needs of this group.

Theory and Literature

Faculty in U.S. institutions of higher education have been studied regularly for determinants of their job satisfaction (Olsen, 1993; Rosser, 2005), as have specific subgroups such as faculty of color and women (Astin, Antonio, Cress, and Astin, 1997; Turner and Myers, 1999). Despite increasing globalization and student demand for international education (Hayward and Siaya, 2001), international faculty have not received similar attention in the United States (Wells and others, forthcoming). Community college international faculty are studied even less frequently, possibly because of their relatively small number.

One salient question for this research concerns potential differences between international and noninternational faculty members in their attitudes, satisfaction, and preferences. Cultural differences based on a connection to, or history in, countries other than the United States may manifest themselves in attitudes and opinions differing from those of people whose primary cultural experiences were in the United States. In other words, are there differences between international and noninternational faculty, other than their country of origin and citizenship? If there are significant differences in attitudes and behaviors, these results will assist institutions in recruiting and retaining an internationalized faculty.

A previous study (Wells and others, forthcoming) explored differences in job satisfaction between international and noninternational faculty members at four-year institutions, and found a mismatch in underlying cultural values between the international faculty and the educational institutions. Using this same framework, I propose that there are likely to be cultural differences between international and noninternational community college faculty manifesting themselves in opinions and attitudes. These differences are important because faculty who have a relatively negative attitude toward their job are more likely to leave the institution, thereby undermining internationalization efforts.

Data and Methods

This study used the 1999 National Study of Postsecondary Faculty dataset, which was compiled by the National Center for Education Statistics. Since these data were collected in 1999, there may be legitimate concern about their relevance in a post–September 11 world. New data are being collected but were unavailable for analysis at the time of publication. Nonetheless, this study is useful for two reasons: it highlights an essentially unstudied group, and it serves as a baseline for future research.

I first compiled a description of the international faculty in community colleges in order to more fully understand this cohort. Second, I used analysis of variance (ANOVA) to determine how international faculty members differed from their noninternational colleagues. After restricting the sample to international faculty at two-year institutions, and weighting the data appropriately, I secured a sample including 357 faculty members at 172 community colleges, which represented 7.6 percent of the total community college faculty members in the dataset (4,675).

Description of the International Faculty

Seventy-five percent of the international faculty members were naturalized citizens, 25 percent were permanent resident immigrants, and 2 percent were temporary resident nonimmigrants. The international faculty was 50 percent male and 50 percent female; 74 percent were married. Approximately 66 percent of international faculty members identified themselves as white, 22 percent identified as Asian, 13 percent as black, and a small percentage as either American Indian or Pacific Islander. Across all racial categories, 23 percent of the respondents reported their ethnicity as Hispanic or Latino.

Most of the international faculty members were originally from Europe (26 percent) and Latin America (25 percent). Additionally, 15 percent of the international faculty were from Asia, 10 percent from the Middle East or North Africa, 6 percent from sub-Saharan Africa, and 3 percent from Oceania. The top five individual countries of origin were the United Kingdom, Mexico, Iran, India, and Germany.

Twenty-three percent of this cohort earned a doctorate, and 57 percent have a master's degree. The top five disciplines in which international faculty teach are mathematics or statistics, education, nursing, business administration, and Spanish. More international faculty work part-time (64.4 percent) than full-time (35.6 percent). Not surprisingly given the predominance of part-time international faculty, 67.4 percent of international faculty members are not tenured. Only 22.6 percent of international faculty

New Directions for Community Colleges • DOI: 10.1002/cc

have tenure, and another 10 percent are on the tenure track. The prevalence of part-time and nontenured status for international faculty may be a significant factor affecting opinions and satisfaction and deserves further attention, but that is beyond the scope of this chapter.

International faculty are not evenly distributed across the United States. Most are located in the West (36.5 percent) followed by the Southwest (16.2 percent), the Mideast (15.0 percent), the Great Lakes region (13.2 percent), and the Southeast (11.0 percent). Smaller percentages are found in the Rocky Mountains (4.8 percent), New England (1.9 percent), and the Plains (1.4 percent). This indicates that certain regions of the United States will have to make a more concerted effort if they hope to substantially internationalize their faculty.

Attitudes and Satisfaction of the International Faculty

The survey used to collect data asked several questions about international faculty attitudes, opinions, and desires. For the purposes of this chapter, these findings are meaningful only if this cohort's means responses (via ANOVA) are distinctly different from the mean responses given by noninternational faculty (significance level less than .10). A few highlights of these findings are presented here (tables of complete results are available on request).

On average, international faculty were more satisfied with their job security than noninternational faculty, but they were less satisfied with their job overall. International faculty were more likely to leave their current job to accept a position at another institution in the next three years, although they were less likely to retire in the next three years. International faculty members were, on average, more likely to leave their job for a number of reasons, among them job security, advancement opportunity, geographic location, and teaching opportunity.

One alarming result of this study concerns opinions about the treatment of minority faculty at U.S. community colleges. A greater proportion of international faculty than noninternational faculty perceived the community college working environment as "less than fair and equitable" for minority groups. Despite these findings, international faculty members were still more likely than noninternational faculty to state that they would choose an academic career again.

Discussion and Implications

To adapt a question posed by Welch (1997), are the differences between international and noninternational faculty due to the failure of international workers to adapt to the local collegial culture, or to an institutional failure to adapt to faculty who bring different perspectives and values? Given the benefits of international education, I propose that the burden of resolving such differences in job attitude rests with the community college. This claim may be met with resistance because a focus on international faculty in recruitment and retention efforts may cost more, and some individuals may perceive negative effects of an internationalized faculty on the basis of superficial characteristics (such as "foreign" accent or behavior).

However, the value of an internationalized faculty outweighs perceived limitations. Students who receive an internationalized education may obtain global literacy (Biddle, 2002) or transnational competence (Hawkins and Cummings, 2000), which can give them an advantage in a globalized job market (Knight, 2004). There is also evidence that students who are exposed to diversity in college show an increase in student learning and growth (Gurin, Nagda, and Lopez, 2004; Pascarella, 2001). In addition, international faculty members increase campus diversity by bringing with them an array of perspectives and experience.

This chapter is a brief introduction to help community college leaders better understand international faculty. Most notably, administrators must acknowledge the fact that international faculty differ from noninternational faculty in their opinions about the treatment of minorities on campus. Regardless of the root causes of this difference (future research on this question is worthwhile), the fact that perceptions differ means that policies, procedures, and training must be examined for fairness and equity.

International faculty reported less overall satisfaction with their job than noninternational faculty, but they were more likely to report they would choose an academic career if they had it to do over again. These results appear contradictory at first glance. However, if international faculty are more mobile than their noninternational colleagues—evidenced by higher likelihood of leaving their job within three years—these findings may be compatible. If dissatisfied, international faculty may be more willing or able to leave in search of a new academic job. In other words, even though they are currently dissatisfied, they may feel that they can still be happy in an academic career if they find an institution that is a better fit.

This study suggests several avenues for future research. The data were collected in 1999; the government has since revised immigration regulations, including those pertaining to international faculty. This study can be useful as a baseline to compare against post–September 11 data. Future research might examine how the post–September 11 climate has changed the opinions, attitudes, and satisfaction of international faculty. In addition, this study only scratches the surface of potential differences between international and noninternational faculty. More rigorous statistical techniques could be applied to many dependent variables, such as job satisfaction, which might tease out the relationship between job satisfaction and part-time or nontenure status. There are also many opportunities to conduct qualitative studies that could explore the underlying reasons for these findings and alternative definitions of "international" faculty membership.

Although a true commitment from all community colleges to internationalization has not been realized, many colleges are genuinely attempting to give their students a high-quality internationalized education. For institutions seeking to bring an international perspective to the classroom and a diversity of international experiences on campus, the global diversity inherent in more international faculty may be a first step. However, if these institutions hope to recruit and retain international faculty they must better understand the satisfaction, opinions, and attitudes of this group, as well as the differences between international and noninternational faculty members on their campus.

References

Astin, H., Antonio, A., Cress, C., and Astin, A. *Race and Ethnicity in the American Professoriate.* Los Angeles: Higher Education Research Institute, University of California, Los Angeles, 1997.

Biddle, S. *Internationalization: Rhetoric or Reality?* New York: American Council of Learned Societies, 2002.

Chase, A. M., and Mahoney, J. R. (eds.). *Global Awareness in Community Colleges: A Report of a National Survey.* Washington, D.C.: Community College Press, 1996.

Gurin, P., Nagda, B. A., and Lopez, G. E. "The Benefits of Diversity in Education for Democratic Citizenship." *Journal of Social Issues,* 2004, *60*(1), 17–34.

Hawkins, J. N., and Cummings, W. K. (eds.). *Transnational Competence: Rethinking the US-Japan Educational Relationship.* Albany: State University of New York Press, 2000.

Hayward, F., and Siaya, L. *Public Experience, Attitudes, and Knowledge: A Report on Two National Surveys About International Education.* Washington, D.C.: American Council on Education, 2001.

Knight, J. "Internationalization Remodeled: Definition, Approaches, and Rationales." *Journal of Studies in International Education,* 2004, *8*(1), 5–31.

Olsen, D. "Work Satisfaction and Stress in the First and Third Year of Academic Appointment." *Journal of Higher Education,* 1993, *64*(4), 453–471.

Pascarella, E. T. "Cognitive Growth in College: Surprising and Reassuring Findings from the National Study of Student Learning." *Change,* Nov.–Dec. 2001, 21–27.

Rosser, V. J. "Measuring the Change in Faculty Perceptions over Time: An Examination of Their Worklife and Satisfaction." *Research in Higher Education,* 2005, *46*(1), 81–107.

Siaya, L., and Hayward, F. *Mapping Internationalization on U.S. Campuses: Final Report.* Washington, D.C.: American Council on Education, 2003.

Turner, C., and Myers, S. *Faculty of Color in Academe: Bittersweet Success.* Needham Heights, Mass.: Allyn and Bacon, 1999.

Welch, A. "The Peripatetic Professor: The Internationalization of the Academic Profession." *Higher Education in Europe,* 1997, *24*(3), 323–345.

Wells, R., Seifert, T., Park, S., Reed, E., and Umbach, P. "Job Satisfaction of International Faculty in U.S. Higher Education." *Journal of the Professoriate,* forthcoming.

RYAN WELLS *is a Ph.D. candidate in educational policy and leadership studies at the University of Iowa.*

10

This chapter presents a case study of challenges that the Peralta Community College District faced in institutionalizing its international student program and describes how the district overcame these challenges.

Campus Politics and the Challenges of International Education in an Urban Community College District

Jacob Ng

Globalization compels community colleges to internationalize their campus to better meet the educational needs of students. To accomplish this task, community colleges must reexamine their educational mission and leadership structure, and determine how to best develop students to be competent global citizens (Selby and Pike, 2000). However, internationalization of community colleges is difficult; campus politics and the conflicting agendas of governing boards, administrators, and international education directors serve as significant barriers to internationalization.

Because education is a highly politicized institution, educational reforms fail or succeed more often for political reasons than for technical issues (Uline, 2001). The same is true for community college international education (Altbach, 2004; Baker, 2006); politics can create barriers that curtail or eliminate programs. This chapter details the political ordeal that the Peralta Community College District's (PCCD) International Education program experienced between 2001 and 2006 and describes how the college dealt with the conflict. The chapter concludes with strategies and recommendations for other campuses facing similar obstacles.

The author would like to thank Daniel Cross for his support in writing this chapter.

International Education at PCCD

The urban communities that PCCD serves are located in Alameda County, California, one of the most culturally diverse counties in the country. PCCD consists of four community colleges: the College of Alameda, Berkeley City College, Laney College, and Merritt College. PCCD's International Education Program has been shaped by a number of global influences and was negatively affected by the events of September 11, 2001, severe acute respiratory syndrome (SARS), war in the Middle East, and immigration reform. Complicating these global influences were internal political conflicts caused by changes in district leadership.

Prior to 1995, PCCD did not have an officially recognized international program. There was no central office where international students could go with issues related to academics, immigration, or college admissions. International student support services of this type are critical because most students come from countries whose cultural needs differ greatly from those of the local domestic population. Moreover, none of the four colleges had the same criteria for admitting international students, and one college was not authorized to enroll them. Given the situation, it was clear that PCCD needed to establish a districtwide service center to meet the specific needs of international students. In 1995, blueprints for a PCCD International Education Program were presented to the district chancellor. Unfortunately, the chancellor's policy advisory council did not see the need for international students, or for a budget to create an international center, support additional staff, and pay for recruitment and travel expenses.

In spring 1997, the idea for a PCCD International Education Program was revitalized and approved by a new chancellor. PCCD became one of the first California community college districts to have a centralized district division responsible for international education. The newly formed Office of International and Global Education's responsibilities were to establish vision and mission statements; oversee international student recruitment, admissions, and advising; provide support services to international students; offer study abroad for domestic students; create faculty and administrative exchanges; internationalize the college curriculum; and develop international ties with overseas institutions and organizations. It also allowed PCCD to efficiently adapt to immigration reforms and tracking requirements introduced shortly after September 11, 2001.

The office's initial emphasis was on international student recruitment. During its first year, the program enrolled roughly one hundred international students. Even though the program was self-supporting, it served these students with just one manager and an administrative assistant. To increase the number of international students at PCCD, the office embarked on a defined recruitment effort and established guidelines and procedures in accordance with immigration rules and regulations. Despite initial logistical challenges, the number of international students grew consistently

NEW DIRECTIONS FOR COMMUNITY COLLEGES • DOI: 10.1002/cc

between 1997 and 2001. By 2002, the program enrolled seven hundred students per semester, placing PCCD in the top thirty community colleges highlighted in the Open Doors Report from the Institute of International Education (Koh Chin, 2003).

Between 1999 and 2002, PCCD's chancellor and governing board members began to show interest in the program and started to travel overseas to promote the program and establish relationships with international institutions and government officials. The chancellor and trustees were instrumental in signing partnership agreements and memos of understanding with their counterparts at overseas institutions. Having board members travel overseas is a positive step for international education; it not only helps to emphasize the importance of international education to the college community but also sends a strong message to overseas partners regarding the seriousness of the college's intent (Blair, Phinney, and Phillippe, 2001). In many countries, it is critical for high-ranking college representatives to broker partnerships.

However, there remained stakeholders at PCCD who did not support international education and were particularly suspicious of international travel. These individuals had a different political agenda from those who supported the program and met with the local press to discuss their criticisms. The critics accused board members of lavishly spending public resources on recruitment trips and international travel; they cited the college for failing to adequately serve international students. For the next three years, the local media scrutinized and negatively attacked all aspects of the International Education Program.

In 2003, a new chancellor was hired who was wary of being involved with the international program. Shortly after being hired, he placed a moratorium on all board member travel. At the same time, districtwide budget cuts and a change in the governing board membership added to the challenges the International Education Program was already facing.

Challenges During Times of Transition

International education programs have faced a number of challenges in recent years. Issues related to war, stricter visa policies, the high cost of living, safety and transportation issues, and increased competition have all served as roadblocks to international education (Baker, 2006). Internal challenges, such as competition for budget allocations, funding for administrative and staff support, and personality conflicts, also exist. However, institutional policies, which can be a defining factor in a program's success or failure, have been ignored within the literature. Sadly, politics often focuses on the needs of individuals rather than the overall mission of the college. It is this aspect of institutional politics that was most challenging to PCCD's international education efforts.

Competing Interests Among District and College Administration. Control over a college program is often quite complicated. In a four-college district, debate over centralized versus decentralized control predominates. Centralized control can be positive, but the district office has to maintain a certain degree of balance with local campuses. At the same time, the success of a central office depends on an understanding that it is ultimately responsible for all of the program's components. At PCCD, for example, the admission process is centralized for international students; all students, regardless of the college to which they apply, must complete the district's international student application. International student applications and visa status are supervised by the Office of International Affairs and Education, which also oversees international program and planning at all four campuses.

Though this setup is efficient, competing interests can complicate the centralization process. For example, debate over centralization exploded when one college administrator recruited international students to his college instead of to all four colleges. This administrator modified the district's international student application by removing three of the college's names, working with a third-party recruiting organization, lobbying for a special acceptance process for his students, and disregarding commonly practiced acceptance procedures and timelines. In the end, thirty-five students who were issued an I-20 form from that particular college were denied visas because proper policies and procedures were not followed. This incident caused the district to lose valuable time and resources, and it affected the reputation of PCCD's International Education Program.

Competing Philosophies. Competing philosophies about the type of student who should be admitted also create challenges for international education programs. At some institutions, there are policymakers who believe international students are a liability and take seats away from deserving domestic students. Unfortunately, these critics fail to recognize that international students bring a wealth of cultural diversity and an exchange of international ideas to the campus. In addition, PCCD international students bring approximately $2.5 million each year in tuition, which sustains the international program and yields an additional $2 million in revenue to support other district programs and services. Two international students in a classroom are enough to financially help support the hiring of one part-time faculty member. International students are also instrumental in saving courses and departments that suffer from budget cuts during times of economic crisis.

Political Aspirations. Political aspirations also proved to be a challenge for districtwide International Education Programs. Although PCCD's program doubled in size between 1997 and 2001, terrorist attacks, the SARS outbreak, and visa regulation changes negatively affected international student programs across the country (Koh Chin, 2005). During this difficult time, PCCD's international program budget was cut, which resulted in lowered student enrollment, loss of three staff members, and diminished support services. Ironically, administrators who supported the budget cuts also expected international student enrollment to increase. Sadly, when enrollment dwindled support for the international program diminished.

NEW DIRECTIONS FOR COMMUNITY COLLEGES • DOI: 10.1002/cc

The political challenges that resulted in budget cuts were further exacerbated by stakeholders who had never supported the international program. Without cause or evidence, local politicians and journalists began to critique PCCD's overseas recruitment efforts. Stories of luxurious travel to distant lands circulated, and the international program was defamed. The program's accomplishments were overlooked; the media focused only on declining international student enrollment, ignoring the influence of major world events. During this period, one board member gained public acclaim for these attacks and used the notoriety to win a city council seat. In 2005, another trustee went even further by attacking the program's administrative leadership. Given that all of these accusations were found to be biased and untrue, the chancellor intervened and the trustee was censured for unprofessional behavior. Nonetheless, these political attacks were damaging to the office's reputation and ability to successfully internationalize the campus.

Strategies for Overcoming Such Challenges

Despite facing intense challenges, the International Education Program administrators worked to regain confidence and rebuild trust with colleagues across the country. Support from the chancellor was essential in defending the integrity and importance of PCCD's international program. Despite his initial reluctance to become involved in the situation, the chancellor dispelled rumors that plagued the district's international program. He made transparency a priority by preparing a public report that explained the vision, mission, functions, and successes of the Office of International Affairs. The chancellor also called on high-level administrators from around the district to support this report by showing the impact international education had made on their individual campuses in terms of services rendered, financial profitability, and addition to their annual budgets. Finally, the chancellor rebutted inaccurate facts concerning international travel and recruitment of international students. He clarified claims of lavish spending (original claims were reported in foreign currencies instead of U.S. dollars) and presented these reports to the board of trustees, ultimately silencing the critics.

International education staff also played a critical role in surviving all these challenges. The staff were united and able to draw strength from one another. This has enabled them to prepare reports and presentations with crucial precision in a very short period of time.

Present State of Affairs

Although PCCD's Office of International Affairs is still facing a number of challenges related to heavy workload, there has been an increase in international student enrollment along with growth in other international projects. Despite vocal opposition to hiring new staff, some supporters in the district want to see the program grow. However, the opposition is strong. Recently, a faculty union leader stated that PCCD's International Education Program had been "running a scam operation all of these years." He is opposed to international student recruitment because international students "hardly speak English and they enroll in my class and they are not good students." This comment is indicative of a context in which international student programs are both desired and reviled.

Future Directions

Recently, PCCD's chancellor presented a series of goals for the international program. One is to strengthen recruitment of international students in an effort to increase enrollment. However, reaching this goal amid current challenges requires the international education staff to be strategic and think carefully about the necessary resources and the political climate. To this end, PCCD's international education office has maintained complete transparency with the board of trustees and college administrators. Furthermore, the office is working to secure funds to build a better infrastructure for international students at all four campuses. Perhaps, after all the challenges that PCCD's Office of International Affairs has faced, there may be reason to believe that the climate is changing. Recently, international education administrators successfully fought to include global and international perspectives in the district's sustainability policy. In addition, the number of domestic students who study abroad has risen. This is a significant step toward internationalization of the district, and it may be a sign that PCCD has successfully weathered the attacks on international students, international education, and its relevance to the community college curriculum.

References

Altbach, P. G. "Higher Education Crosses Borders." *Change,* Mar.–Apr. 2004, 1–12.

Baker, A. L. "Advocacy—Five Years Later." *International Educator,* 2006, *15,* 4–6.

Blair, D., Phinney, L., and Phillippe, K. A. "International Programs at Community Colleges." AACC Research Brief no. AACC-RB-01-1. Washington, D.C.: American Association of Community Colleges, 2001.

Koh Chin, H. K. *Open Doors: Report on International Educational Exchange.* New York: Institute of International Education, 2003.

Koh Chin, H. K. *Open Doors: Report on International Educational Exchange.* New York: Institute of International Education, 2005.

Selby, D., and Pike, G. "Civil Global Education: Relevant Learning for the Twenty-First Century." *Convergence,* 2000, *33*(1–2), 138–149.

Uline, C. L. "The Imperative to Change." *International Journal of Leadership in Education,* 2001, *4,* 13–28.

JACOB NG founded the Peralta Community College District International Education Program and currently serves as the district's associate vice chancellor for international affairs.

11

This chapter offers a case study of Kapi'olani Community College, an institution that initiated its Asia-Pacific emphasis in 1988, strengthened the emphasis throughout the 1990s, and expanded it to an integrated international emphasis in 2007.

Island Roots, Global Reach: A Case Study in Internationalizing Kapi'olani Community College

Leon Richards, Robert W. Franco

With an enrollment of 7,289 students, Kapi'olani* Community College (KCC) is the largest two-year college in the ten campus University of Hawai'i system. KCC's location on the slopes of Diamond Head affords a unique vantage point. It looks east to the sunrise and distant America and west to the Honolulu city lights, Pearl Harbor, and distant Oceania and Asia. The college bears the name of Queen Julia Kapi'olani, who was deeply committed to the health and education of her people. Her motto *Kulia i ka Nu'u*, which means to strive for the highest, inspires the college's collective work in support of academic success for native Hawai'ian and other local and international students. In fall 2006, approximately 70 percent of enrolled students were Asian; 12 percent were Caucasian; 10 percent were Hawai'ian; and 8.3 percent were Pacific Islander, Hispanic, African American, or of mixed ethnic background. International enrollments climbed to 563; 75 percent were from Japan or South Korea. Nearly six in ten of all students were female, and the student mean age was 24.8 years.

KCC offers a strong precollege developmental education program; the largest liberal arts and transfer program in the University of Hawai'i System;

---

*Kapi'olani is a Hawai'ian word with Latin vowel sounds. The diacritical mark indicates a break in pronunciation, that is, "Kapi-olani."

NEW DIRECTIONS FOR COMMUNITY COLLEGES, no. 138, Summer 2007 © 2007 Wiley Periodicals, Inc.
Published online in Wiley InterScience (www.interscience.wiley.com) • DOI: 10.1002/cc.286

a statewide nursing and health science training center; and quality training programs in biotechnology, exercise and sports science, hotel operations, travel and tourism, culinary arts, business, legal assisting, new media arts, and teacher preparation. The college's general education and transfer program is articulated to the University of Hawai'i at Manoa, a major research university. To create a unique and coherent educational experience for its students, KCC developed *across-the-curriculum emphases* that have shaped faculty recruitment and development, curricular focus and enhancement, and resource development for nearly twenty years. Historically, the first of these emphases was Writing and Critical Thinking, followed by the Asia-Pacific, Information Technology, and Service Learning Emphases.

Kapi'olani Asia-Pacific Emphasis (KAPE)

Since 1986, KCC has been developing and refining the Asia-Pacific Emphasis in an effort to strengthen the general education program and expand the worldview of island-bound students. This emphasis was chosen on the basis of Hawai'i's unique geographic, demographic, cultural, and linguistic position in relation to Asia and the Pacific Islands. Faculty chose to emphasize Asian, Pacific, and American connectedness rather than Hawai'i as remote and isolated. The emphasis builds on the diverse backgrounds of our students, faculty, and community; the expertise of faculty trained at the University of Hawai'i, Manoa, a leader in Asian, Hawai'ian, and Pacific Islands Studies; and the East-West Center, a major federal research center with a mandate to support partnerships, peace, and prosperity in the Asia-Pacific region. Two core principles drive the Kapi'olani Asia-Pacific Emphasis. First, the college seeks to serve as a bridge among Asia, the Pacific, and the Americas; and second, all programs should be student-centered, faculty-driven, and administration-supported.

In 2001, KCC was selected to participate in an American Council on Education (ACE) national initiative called Promising Practices in Institutionalizing International Education. Participation in this initiative required development and implementation of a comprehensive audit of the extent to which the Asia-Pacific Emphasis was institutionalized. This internal audit was supplemented by an external evaluation conducted by a team of ACE international education experts. As a result of these evaluations, ACE suggested that the college broaden its geographic and cultural lens to include the Americas, Africa, and the Middle East. From 2003 to the present, the Asia-Pacific Emphasis has evolved into the Integrated International Emphasis (IIE), which connects KCC's indigenous and intercultural roots with its international reach extending to and beyond Asia and the Pacific.

NEW DIRECTIONS FOR COMMUNITY COLLEGES • DOI: 10.1002/cc

Current State of Knowledge: Internationalizing the Institution and Student Learning

As a result of Promising Practices and ongoing research through their international collaborative, ACE developed six principles for effective institutionalization; these principles frame the discussion here of international education at Kapi'olani (Engberg and Green, 2002).

An Integrative and Comprehensive Approach. The opportunities for critical inquiry stimulated by comparative indigenous, intercultural, and international education constitute a continuous impetus to further internationalization at KCC. The college's shared vision of internationalization challenges the institution to support the languages, cultures, and histories of Hawai'i's people; strengthen students' capacity to understand and respect diverse cultures; develop strong educational and economic partnerships in Asia, the Pacific, and the Americas; and increase access to and success in its academic programs. Specifically, goal four of the college's strategic plan seeks to foster diversity in local, regional, and global learning and suggests that the classroom, campus, and community offer a spectrum of indigenous, intercultural, and international experiences that enhance student learning and faculty development. To make the strategic plan a reality, the college is working to weave the IIE through all academic, transfer, and cocurricular programs, community- and Internet-based learning opportunities, and study abroad.

Strong Leadership at the Top. In the late 1980s and throughout the 1990s, Joyce Tsunoda, chancellor of the University of Hawai'i (UH) Community Colleges, supported the shared vision and brought administrative support to help students better understand Asian and Pacific cultures. Additionally, under the leadership of a visionary chancellor and vice-chancellor for academic affairs, KCC continued to promote and develop international and intercultural education as a tool to prepare students for lives as socially responsible and economically productive members of their communities. In response to a rapidly revitalizing Native Hawai'ian culture and community that is reasserting its traditional cultural values, beliefs, and sovereignty, this leadership team, along with empowered faculty, also developed an indigenous Hawai'ian focus that roots the work of the institution in the values of Queen Kapi'olani and the culture she represents (Colby and Ehrlich, 2003; Morton and Franco, 2004).

Committed Leadership and Widespread Faculty Engagement. The college's core principle of being student-centered, faculty-driven, and administration-supported has also helped to promote international education. The chancellor's office imparts substantial vision, leadership, and funding for a number of international initiatives. The vice-chancellor for academic affairs, who oversees international education and international institutional partnerships, brings financial support to the faculty who lead the international education programs.

For most of its history, the Kapi'olani Asia-Pacific Emphasis, now known as the IIE, has been coordinated by two faculty members who each receive one course release per semester. One of these faculty members takes primary responsibility for coordinating the International Education Week in November and the International Festival Week in March. Now in its nineteenth year, the International Festival features a lecture and film series, student presentations, student club activities, and a vibrant program of performing and visual arts. Events are synchronized with spring course syllabi and scheduled to maximize student participation. The festival also attracts hundreds of community members to campus and helps build strong intercultural partnerships with numerous local ethnic organizations and community stakeholders. Faculty members also direct development of a campus environment that reflects the college's vision and commitment to indigenous, intercultural, and international understanding. For example, all buildings on the campus are named after indigenous Hawai'ian plants, and botany students help cultivate Hawai'ian plants on campus and work at a millennial peace garden adjacent to the campus.

Recruitment and retention of faculty (who have completed advanced degrees at the University of Hawai'i or conducted research at the East-West Center) has also contributed to the strength of the program. Additionally, the college has successfully cultivated intellectual breadth and depth in its faculty by funding faculty development and study abroad. Nearly 40 percent of the faculty have participated in planning, implementing, and evaluating IIE; 60 percent of all courses offered include Hawai'ian, Pacific, Asian, and international content and context.

Supportive Structures and Resources. Three distinct structures with well-defined roles and responsibilities support integrated international education at KCC: the Malama Hawai'i Center, the Honda International Center, and the planning and grants development office. The Malama Hawai'i Center supports Native Hawai'ian student access and success in an environment that integrates Hawai'ian values with student support services, faculty-student interaction, and active and collaborative learning. Native Hawai'ian faculty members have developed a rich curriculum and strong pedagogy focusing on Hawai'ian culture, language, history, and contemporary issues. These Native Hawai'ian faculty members have also created faculty development workshops that discuss the aforementioned topics so that the concepts can be integrated into the general education curriculum and campus culture. With the leadership and coordination of Malama Hawai'i faculty, some Native Hawai'ian students have completed two reciprocal study abroad programs to New Zealand to learn from their close relatives, the Maori people. New funds from the National Science Foundation will enable closer interactions with students and faculty in Samoa and Micronesia.

The Honda International Center (HIC) is a comprehensive center for all international students, providing enrollment management and student transition services. The center supports local and international workforce

NEW DIRECTIONS FOR COMMUNITY COLLEGES • DOI: 10.1002/cc

development and training partnerships in promising new fields. For example, the HIC develops customized contract training programs that range from two-day Pacific Rim and Hawai'ian regional cuisine demonstrations to four-week intensive English language and American and Hawai'ian culture training, to sixteen-week English as a second language teacher training.

The HIC also helps to develop the capacity of local students to understand and respect diverse cultures by implementing study abroad opportunities. Currently, the HIC maintains international agreements with fifty colleges and universities, which together bring students a variety of study abroad opportunities. These agreements and partnerships also serve as the basis for international customized contract training and education. The HIC also collaborates with the Japanese Consul in Hawai'i to administer three-year, fully funded Monbugakusho Scholarships for study abroad. Additionally, the college has been awarded $2.4 million from the Freeman Foundation to offer intensive second language instruction, study abroad, and international service learning opportunities in China, Japan, and Korea. Now in its third year, this generous grant has fully funded sixty UH Community College Freeman Scholars while they study for one semester at KCC and another semester abroad.

The planning and grants development office, which has successfully garnered external resources for the ongoing development of IIE, is the third supportive structure at KCC. These grants consistently support needed improvements as identified by the faculty and administration.

Commitment to Student Needs. The college's commitment to meeting student needs is manifest in its comprehensive general education and liberal arts program. The first component of this program is a set of courses that meet the University of Hawai'i Manoa (UHM) Global and Multicultural Foundations general education requirement. Students are required to take two courses that present interdisciplinary perspectives on world history and geography as well as religious, artistic, and cultural developments. Within the general education program, students can also complete Hawai'ian, Asian, and international studies academic certificates comprising courses that all meet general education, degree, and transfer requirements. The Asian and international studies certificates have specified learning outcomes developed in collaboration with ACE's ongoing Lessons Learned in Assessing International Learning.

With U.S. Department of Education Title VIA funding, KCC is developing an international studies certificate with new courses that are thematic and comparative. One new course is entitled Islam in Africa, the Middle East, and Asia; another is Art in Africa, the Americas, and Oceania. A third course focuses on global environmental issues, and a fourth examines Latin American literature; the latter course complements existing American and Asian literature courses. A fifth course gives students insight into contemporary Middle East politics and complements a rich set of existing intercultural and international courses. The final Title VIA curriculum component is development of an intensive content-based Spanish language course that will enable students to complete the existing two-year Spanish course sequence in one year. This intensive, content-based Spanish curriculum parallels existing courses in Chinese, Japanese, and Korean. To add further coherence to the international studies academic subject certificate, these newly developed courses share common themes and issues such as religion and conflict; technology and globalization; populations and health; and languages, literature, and identity.

All students must complete a one-year second language requirement for the associate degree in liberal arts. Hundreds of students complete this language requirement annually and continue to complete second-year language study to meet UH Manoa baccalaureate requirements. This requirement leads to strong faculty collaboration in the Second Language Development and Teaching (SLDT) Department. The SLDT faculty have developed intensive content-based second language learning courses in Japanese, Chinese, and Korean. The SLDT faculty have also developed strong curriculum for non-English speakers, and for students interested in second languages for specific purposes. Our international students and limited English speakers are encouraged and supported to develop their native languages through Language in Application courses. In these courses, first language speakers apply their language knowledge and skills through service learning and tutoring to support faculty teaching second language learners preparing for careers in tourism, business, and health.

The college also has a unique Understanding Self and Community general education standard with learning outcomes focused on cultural and linguistic diversity and ethical and civic responsibility. Each semester, forty courses connect 250 students to intercultural and intergenerational service-learning opportunities in Honolulu's diverse ethnic communities (Colby and Ehrlich, 2003). Since 1995, seven thousand students have successfully completed service-learning and civic responsibility assignments. Students and faculty work in schools and community-based organizations to understand and appreciate the Hawai'ian genius for environmental productivity and sustainability, and the diverse linguistic and cultural backgrounds of immigrant families. For example, through the Palolo Pipeline Project students tutor new immigrant children from Southeast Asia and the Pacific Islands, along with encouraging these students' parents to return to college. Through Project SHINE, students help elderly Chinese immigrants prepare for the U.S. citizenship test and stand beside these respected elders as they are ceremonially sworn in as American citizens. In 2006, students and faculty from Kapi'olani Community College, the University of Hawai'i Manoa, St. Mary's University in Texas, and Park University participated in a Global Solutions Project funded by ACE. Over a two-week period, students and faculty studied in the Palolo Valley. Through their work, they developed a Healthy Communities Website that published relevant health information to communities around the world.

Three other campus innovations demonstrate the college's commitment to meeting student needs. Through International Café, students from all cultures meet in a casual café setting to share their talents in a structured service learning initiative. Language exchanges and tutoring are two of the most popular features of the International Café, along with student presentations and cultural activities. The International Café and related service-learning activities are based on the premise that every student has something to teach as well as to learn. For example, seventy local and international students recently spent Martin Luther King Day renovating five retired tour buses so they could be used as transitional shelter for Hawai'i's homeless. This service project was contextualized with the knowledge and expertise of a homeless shelter director and reflected on in three liberal arts courses and the International Café. International Café activities are also being replicated by partner institutions in Japan and Korea.

The second innovation is the International Seminar, which is embedded within the English for speakers of other languages (ESOL 197) program, an intensive English program designed to help nonnative speakers of English succeed in mainstream college-level classes. In this program, local students, faculty, and counselors work with nonnative speakers in weekly seminars; discussion topics include culture shock and adaptation, survival tips while studying in Hawai'i, the American higher educational system, and baccalaureate transfer.

The third innovation is coordinated by the Access to College Excellence program. In this program, international students and local students are registered in the same classes to facilitate academic and cultural exchange. Active student involvement in the International Café, the International Seminar Program, and the Access to College Excellence initiative brings international cultural diversity to life and to learning.

Assessing International Learning Outcomes. KCC is currently working with five other colleges and universities to develop knowledge, skills, and attitudinal outcomes expected of the globally competent student. The project has also developed a student e-portfolio system that captures student background data (variables hypothesized to affect international learning) that can be correlated with learning artifacts posted to their e-portfolio. In addition, the project has developed instructions for students to follow in developing their e-portfolio, and training handbooks for faculty e-portfolio raters. Thus far, eight of the Freeman Scholars have created e-portfolios that capture learning outcomes from their intensive language learning and study abroad as well as from additional courses taken in Asian and international studies.

An Asian studies course matrix also aligns individual course competencies with the learning outcomes. Faculty are being encouraged to focus on "assignment alignment" so that their course assignments more explicitly direct students to produce evidence of expected learning outcomes (Olson, Green, and Hill, 2006). The student international e-portfolio methodology is in its incipient stage and has not yet generated outcomes assessment data. Kapi'olani faculty who are involved in the project are disseminating campus developments via the ACE International Collaborative, International Studies

Association, Association of International Education Administrators, and American Association of Community Colleges annual conferences.

Conclusion

As a result of ACE-driven institutional assessments of international education, and its own recognition of the college's unique responsibilities to Hawai'ian students, KCC is simultaneously deepening and expanding its indigenous, intercultural, international, and globalization curriculum and programs. The years ahead will require a slight shift in one of the college's core principles: it must move from student-centered to learner-centered while continuing to be faculty-driven and administration-supported. The college is delivering on its mission to prepare students for rigorous baccalaureate requirements, and for lives as economically productive and socially responsible members of their communities. We have identified our strengths and weaknesses, and we have developed new planning, assessment, and budgeting cycles to support ongoing improvement. Like every community college, KCC is meeting the needs and shaping the dreams of its students; we are carefully crafting tactics and strategies so that all students learn to succeed in a rapidly changing world.

References

Colby, A., and Ehrlich, T. *Educating Citizens: Preparing America's Undergraduates for Lives of Civic and Moral Responsibility.* San Francisco: Jossey-Bass, 2003.

Engberg, D., and Green, M. *Promising Practices: Spotlighting Excellence in Comprehensive Internationalization.* Washington, D.C.: American Council on Education, 2002.

Morton, J., and Franco, R. "Social Responsibility in 21st Century Hawai'i: Kapiolani as Engaged Campus." *AAC&U Peer Review,* Winter 2004, 28–30.

Olson, C., Green, M., and Hill, B. *A Handbook for Comprehensive Internationalization: What Institutions Can Do and What Students Should Learn.* Washington, D.C.: American Council on Education, 2006.

LEON RICHARDS *is acting chancellor and executive director for international education for University of Hawai'i-Kapi'olani Community College.*

ROBERT W. FRANCO *is professor of anthropology and director of planning and grants development at University of Hawai'i-Kapi'olani Community College.*

NEW DIRECTIONS FOR COMMUNITY COLLEGES • DOI: 10.1002/cc

INDEX

CC133 **Latino Educational Opportunity**
Catherine L. Horn, Stella M. Flores, Gary Orfield
Latinos enroll at community colleges at rates higher than any other racial or ethnic group. Many factors influence Latino education—immigration policy, language, academic opportunity, family—and, despite research, the influence of these factors remains confounding. This issue explains the ways and extent to which community colleges can provide Latino students with access and opportunity.
ISBN: 0-7879-8624-0

CC132 **Sustaining Financial Support for Community Colleges**
Stephen G. Katsinas, James C. Palmer
Describes institutional approaches for securing adequate funding in an era of recurrent recessions, legislator reluctance to raise taxes, and intense competition for scarce resources. Chapter authors give guidelines for fundraising, corporate partnerships, grants for workforce development, mill levy elections, realigning budget priorities, and the key skills that today's community college presidents need.
ISBN: 0-7879-8364-0

CC131 **Community College Student Affairs: What Really Matters**
Steven R. Helfgot, Marguerite M. Culp
Uses the results of a national survey to identify the major challenges and opportunities for student affairs practitioners in community colleges, and describes the most effective strategies for meeting challenges. Chapters discuss core values, cultures of evidence, faculty partnerships, career counseling, and support for underrepresented populations, plus assessment tools and best practices in student affairs.
ISBN: 0-7879-8332-2

CC130 **Critical Thinking: Unfinished Business**
Christine M. McMahon
With a few exceptions, critical thinking is not being effectively taught nor even correctly understood in higher education. This volume advocates for professional development in critical thinking to engage all members of the campus community. It presents blueprints for such development, plus practical case studies from campuses already doing it. Also covers classroom assignments, solutions to resistance, and program assessment.
ISBN: 0-7879-8185-0

CC129 **Responding to the Challenges of Developmental Education**
Carol A. Kozeracki
Approximately 40 percent of incoming community college students enroll in developmental math, English, or reading courses. Despite the availability of popular models for teaching these classes, community colleges continue to struggle with effectively educating underprepared students, who have a wide variety of backgrounds. This volume discusses the dangers of isolating developmental education from the broader college; provides examples of successful programs; offers recommendations adaptable to different campuses; and identifies areas for future research.
ISBN: 0-7879-8050-1

CC128 **From Distance Education to E-Learning: Lessons Along the Way**
Beverly L. Bower, Kimberly P. Hardy
Correspondence, telecourses, and now e-learning: distance education continues to grow and change. This volume's authors examine what community colleges must do to make distance education successful,

including meeting technology challenges, containing costs, developing campuswide systems, teaching effectively, balancing faculty workloads, managing student services, and redesigning courses for online learning. Includes case studies from colleges, plus state and regional policy perspectives.
ISBN: 0-7879-7927-9

CC127   **Serving Minority Populations**
Berta Vigil Laden
Focuses on how colleges with emerging majority enrollments of African American, Hispanic, American Indian, Asian American and Pacific Islander, and other ethnically diverse students are responding to the needs— academic, financial, and cultural—of their increasingly diverse student populations. Discusses partnerships with universities, businesses, foundations, and professional associations that can increase access, retention, and overall academic success for students of color. Covers best practices from Minority-Serving Institutions, and offers examples for mainstream community colleges.
ISBN: 0-7879-7790-X

CC126   **Developing and Implementing Assessment of Student Learning Outcomes**
Andreea M. Serban, Jack Friedlander
Colleges are under increasing pressure to produce evidence of student learning, but most assessment research focuses on four-year colleges. This volume is designed for practitioners looking for models that community colleges can apply to measuring student learning outcomes at the classroom, course, program, and institutional levels to satisfy legislative and accreditation requirements.
ISBN: 0-7879-7687-3

CC125   **Legal Issues in the Community College**
Robert C. Cloud
Community colleges must be prepared for lawsuits, federal statutes, court rulings, union negotiations, and other legal issues that could affect institutional stability and effectiveness. This volume provides leaders with information about board relations, tenure and employment, student rights and safety, disability law, risk management, copyright and technology issues, and more.
ISBN: 0-7879-7482-X

NEW DIRECTIONS FOR COMMUNITY COLLEGES
Order Form
SUBSCRIPTIONS AND SINGLE ISSUES

DISCOUNTED BACK ISSUES:

Use this form to receive **20% off** all back issues of New Directions for Community Colleges. All single issues priced at **$23.20** (normally $29.00)

TITLE   ISSUE NO.   ISBN

_____ _____   _____
_____ _____   _____

Call 888-378-2537 or see mailing instructions below. When calling, mention the promotional code JB7ND to receive your discount.

SUBSCRIPTIONS: *(1 year, 4 issues)*

☐ New Order   ☐ Renewal

U.S.	☐ Individual: $80	☐ Institutional: $195
Canada/Mexico	☐ Individual: $80	☐ Institutional: $235
All Others	☐ Individual: $104	☐ Institutional: $269

Call 888-378-2537 or see mailing and pricing instructions below. Online subscriptions are available at www.interscience.wiley.com.

Copy or detach page and send to:
John Wiley & Sons, Journals Dept, 5th Floor
989 Market Street, San Francisco, CA 94103-1741

Order Form can also be faxed to: 888-481-2665

Issue/Subscription Amount: $ _____	**SHIPPING CHARGES:**		
Shipping Amount: $ _____	SURFACE	Dometic	Canadian
(for single issues only—subscription prices include shipping)	First Item	$5.00	$6.00
Total Amount: $ _____	Each Add'l Item	$3.00	$1.50

(No sales tax for U.S. subscriptions. Canadian residents, add GST for subscription orders. Individual rate subscriptions must be paid by personal check or credit card. Individual rate subscriptions may not be resold as library copies.)

☐ Payment enclosed (U.S. check or money order only. All payments must be in U.S. dollars.)

☐ VISA ☐ MC ☐ Amex # _____ Exp. Date _____

Card Holder Name _____ Card Issue # _____

Signature_____ Day Phone _____

☐ Bill Me (U.S. institutional orders only. Purchase order required.)

Purchase order # _____
                        Federal Tax ID13559302   **GST 89102 8052**

Name _____

Address _____

Phone _____ E-mail _____

JB7ND

**NEW DIRECTIONS FOR COMMUNITY COLLEGES
IS NOW AVAILABLE ONLINE AT WILEY INTERSCIENCE**

What is Wiley InterScience?

Wiley InterScience is the dynamic online content service from John Wiley & Sons delivering the full text of over 300 leading scientific, technical, medical, and professional journals, plus major reference works, the acclaimed *Current Protocols* laboratory manuals, and even the full text of select Wiley print books online.

What are some special features of Wiley InterScience?

Wiley InterScience Alerts is a service that delivers table of contents via e-mail for any journal available on Wiley InterScience as soon as a new issue is published online.
Early View is Wiley's exclusive service presenting individual articles online as soon as they are ready, even before the release of the compiled print issue. These articles are complete, peer-reviewed, and citable.
CrossRef is the innovative multi-publisher reference linking system enabling readers to move seamlessly from a reference in a journal article to the cited publication, typically located on a different server and published by a different publisher.

How can I access Wiley InterScience?

Visit http://www.interscience.wiley.com

Guest Users can browse Wiley InterScience for unrestricted access to journal Tables of Contents and Article Abstracts, or use the powerful search engine.
Registered Users are provided with a *Personal Home Page* to store and manage customized alerts, searches, and links to favorite journals and articles. Additionally, Registered Users can view free Online Sample Issues and preview selected material from major reference works.
Licensed Customers are entitled to access full-text journal articles in PDF, with select journals also offering full-text HTML.

How do I become an Authorized User?

Authorized Users are individuals authorized by a paying Customer to have access to the journals in Wiley InterScience. For example, a university that subscribes to Wiley journals is considered to be the Customer. Faculty, staff and students authorized by the university to have access to those journals in Wiley InterScience are Authorized Users. Users should contact their Library for information on which Wiley journals they have access to in Wiley InterScience.

ASK YOUR INSTITUTION ABOUT WILEY INTERSCIENCE TODAY!

Your guide to serving a new generation of students.

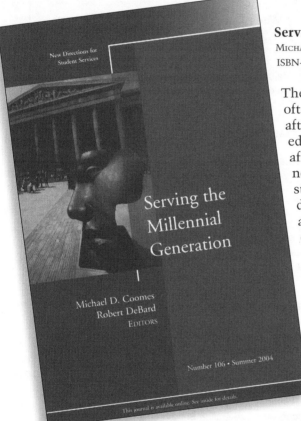

Serving the Millennial Generation
MICHAEL D. COOMES AND ROBERT DeBARD, EDITORS
ISBN-10: 0-7879-7606-7 • $28.00

The Millennial Generation, often categorized as those born after 1981, will require higher education leaders and student affairs practitioners to adopt new learning and service strategies, rethink student development theories, and modify educational environments. *Serving the Millennial Generation* gives readers the foundation for understanding this newest generation of students and to offer suggestions on how to educate and serve them more effectively.

Table of Contents:

Serving the Millennial Generation is a best-selling issue of the quarterly report *New Directions for Student Services*. Subscriptions can be ordered by calling 888-378-2537.